Hope you enjoy
reading my book
Best Wishes

Roy Hall
10/10/2000

UNDER THE MANGO TREE

Roy Hall

MINERVA PRESS
LONDON
MONTREUX LOS ANGELES SYDNEY

UNDER THE MANGO TREE
Copyright © Roy Hall 1998

All Rights Reserved

ISBN 1 86106 807 7

First Published 1998 by
MINERVA PRESS
195 Knightsbridge
London SW7 1RE

Printed in Great Britain for Minerva Press

UNDER THE MANGO TREE

In memory of my mother
Hilda Beatrice Caroline Hall
1910–1984

And for Charles H. Sseggendo, pupils and staff at
Kojcha School for the Deaf, Uganda

*

They are able because they think they are able

Virgil

Acknowledgements

The author gratefully acknowledges the assistance given by his friends Terry Cawtheray, of Blackheath in London, and Jean Moore, at present living in Anguilla, British West Indies, who willingly gave their time to proof read the following pages of this book.

To Shaul Penn at the Kibbutz Yizreel in Israel, for his contribution on the rearing of blind calves.

To Geoff Breeden and scouts of Northumberland, for compiling and sending to me a copy of *Uganda 91*.

By the same author:

Aid To Communication With Signed English

*An Introduction To Children With Special Needs For Teachers
In Mainstream Schools*

Sign Language For Schools

Contents

Chapter One
Under The Mango Tree

Sitting in my office in Africa, under the shade of a mango tree, I often think of the office I left in England a number of years ago. Then I had a friendly secretary to keep me company. Fitted carpets running from wall to wall. Telephones that never failed to work. A word processor, photocopier, air-conditioning and power at the press of a switch. Now I have ants, lizards and stray birds as my daytime companions with cockroaches, rats and bats at night. Grass grows through the mud floor which my chickens like to peck. I have an oil lamp for evenings and an umbrella to keep myself dry during tropical storms and showers.

I am living in Uganda, close to the centre of this vast continent of Africa. Uganda is often referred to as 'The Pearl of Africa', a title used by some explorers during the early days of exploration. The Equator on the map runs through the southern half of the country but in most areas the climate remains pleasant. Mornings and evenings are usually cool with a breeze coming from Lake Victoria. This makes a welcome change for me after suffering many long, hot, sleepless nights in other tropical countries. The lake, once thought by David Livingstone to be the Atlantic Ocean, borders much of the south of Uganda. Rainfall is sufficient most years to allow all crops to survive. Even during the most critical years of civil war few people went hungry because the land was so fertile. People say that you just have to drop a seed in the ground, then sit back and let nature do the rest.

My office walls are made of mud bricks baked by my African son Charles. These are inexpensive and fairly simple to construct but do have a limited life due to the elements and insects. The bricks are made from either loam or clay. Water is mixed with the soil which is then hoed and pounded by bare feet until soft, then covered with grass until dry. The bricks are then shaped in a handmade mould, turned out, stacked to form a kiln, covered with mud and baked for a number of days. Between one thousand and ten thousand bricks are produced at any one time. These have a selling price of 3p to 4p for loam bricks and 5p to 6p for clay.

Building materials are relatively low in price but with so much to construct our money started to run out. The main school block contained a classroom, dormitory, office and toilets. By the time the first children arrived we had not completed all the walls, and toilets remained without doors or a roof. Children used to laugh at me when I walked to the toilets in the rain and mud, sheltering under my large, insect eaten umbrella. I would then gradually ease my aching bones into a squatting position over a hole going down twenty feet beneath me. Sometimes I would wait for the privacy of the dark evening hours. At night I had to hold my pocket torch in my mouth, umbrella in the right hand, with the left used for shooing away cockroaches until it was needed for an additional service.

After a few months more money arrived from friends overseas. We were then able to put into place the final two layers of bricks around the whole of the building, place a roof on the toilet block and have the luxury of squatting behind closed doors. This also meant we could now have both hands free, one to chase away the cockroaches and the other to catch mosquitoes.

My most frequent office visitors are ants wandering from floor to rafters. I usually manage to avoid bites but occasionally one penetrates my clothing and makes a sudden attack in the centre of my back or on the top of my balding head. The feeling is similar to that of a red hot needle being plunged into the body. If I accidentally spill a few grains of sugar then the ants are swarming. There is a saying that if ants were the size of dogs then there would not be sufficient space for people to live on earth. I have seen a wall seething with a mass of crawling blackness. One day I left a book outside on the grass and before being discovered it had been chewed by ants into a pile of dust. I once placed a dead snake in a container without a cover and by the end of the day there remained a pile of bones. It is said that ants in Africa have killed a young baby overnight by smothering it and removing all the flesh. When ants are on the march you can hear the rustle coming towards you through the grass. A well-known Japanese torture was to bury a man in an ant hill up to his neck with just his head showing above the ground. This was a slow agonising killing with the prisoner remaining alive while the ants slowly ate away his body. One morning I saw ten dead ants making their way across the brickwork. On a closer look I saw that it was an insect which specialises in carrying its food on its back and was making towards its lair for a feast.

More friendly visitors to my office are the lizards. They announce their approach by sending an amount of brick or cement crumbling down on to my books or papers. Sometimes these reptiles are almost invisible to the eye but give themselves away by a bump moving behind one of the wall maps or pictures, perhaps making Kilimanjaro seem to have grown to even greater heights. My favourite lizards are the ones with so many bright colours covering the skin that you would think that a child had splashed them with all the colours available in the paint box. Perhaps the most fascinating member of the lizard family is the chameleon, famous for its ability to change colour according to its surroundings. One morning Charles called me into the garden to show me a chameleon he had found resting, as if frozen, on a dead banana leaf. Both leaf and skin were the same tawny brown. When we moved the still motionless creature to a fresh green leaf we observed the quick change of colour taking place to match its new background. The bulging eyes can move independently of each other having the advantage of being able to look two ways at the same time swivelling backwards and forwards. It can, however, focus them together on its insect prey. The club-like sticky tongue can be projected forward six or seven inches, rarely missing its intended target. Much superstition surrounds the chameleon in Africa. I first encountered this in Tanzania. People would not come near one I was carrying and ladies covered their faces and hurried away. It was thought to be evil, mainly because of its ability to see in all directions at the same time, the ever watching all seeing eyes. Fortunately near our mango tree we do not have the largest member of the lizard family, the Komodo dragon, as seen in Indonesia. These monsters can grow to over ten feet in length and would soon eat some of our friendly school goats. I have more than once been woken from a late afternoon doze by two playful lizards missing their footing and dropping down on to me.

Chickens often wander through the ever open door looking for any small morsel carelessly dropped. Standing in one corner of the room is an old jerrycan containing paraffin. The cap was mislaid some time ago and its place has been taken by a very dry maize cob. A colourful decorated cockerel discovered this possible source of food some days ago. Unfortunately for Chauntecleer this maize had passed its sell-by date, being too hard to be broken up by the strongest beak. However, he does not give up and averages six attacks a day on the cob, giving up after a few pecks until the next time. The bird pecks up a few ants as a consolation prize on its way out. Chickens inspecting my office do not disturb me but I do keep them out of the classroom and dormitory and away from the food being prepared and cooked under another of our mango trees. The problem for me with fowls in class or lecture rooms is the disturbance caused by their clucking, crowing, fluttering of wings or hopping from chair to chair. Sometimes the room was silent, with my students waiting to hear how the thirty thousand hairs led from the cochlea to the brain stem, when a cock would crow at a hundred decibels under my table. Helpless laughter would break out and I would say to myself that I never remembered this situation happening during my Manchester days.

Standing in another corner of my office is a bow with two arrows, the property of Adam, our night watchman. He patrols the grounds every night, seven evenings a week, but as far as I know he has never put these weapons to use. In the morning I often ask if he has shot anyone during the night but Adam always smiles and shakes his head. We are fortunate in having an honest and reliable security man. So often the watchman has been the one who has unlocked a door, turned a blind eye or handed over the valuables to his friends on the outside. Theft is certainly a problem. Colleagues once had their transport stolen at gun point. The first indication of trouble was when the driver had a pistol pressed into the side of his head. The director of an organisation I worked for was murdered in front of his family while four thieves drove away in his car. With Uganda having five international borders it is not difficult to steal a vehicle, travel into another country and dispose of a car or truck. Even poor Charles has not escaped this thuggery. One night he was attacked and robbed and left for dead in a ditch at the side of a main road. It was not until the following morning that he was discovered and given the necessary help and treatment.

The rattle of heavy drops of rain on our tin roof reminds me of the frequent nightly gun fire which we used to hear, both at a distance and around our house. Now gunfire might be heard once a month after soldiers have been celebrating for an evening. Fortunately the country is now at peace politically, apart from a few trouble spots close to the borders where rebels are still active. (Before travelling to some of the remoter areas of Uganda it is wise to check with both the tourist office in Parliament Avenue in Kampala and your own high commission or embassy as to the possible dangers of visiting a certain area.) So hopefully we can sleep at night with the belief that Adam will know how to use his bow and arrows if the occasion arises.

This part of the world is a paradise for bird spotters. It often seems that we are living in an aviary of tropical birds at a zoo. So far just one species has entered the office and this is the grey-headed sparrow. He is an inquisitive bird, flying in from the mango tree and perching on one of the roof beams above my desk peering down at me. The greyhead is a larger bird than the British sparrow, with a tawny brown mantle and a head of pale grey, as the name suggests. After a few minutes of hopping around the rafters, this sparrow is soon off again for the shelter of our large tree. From my office window I can see my favourite visitors to the mango tree, a pair of trumpeter hornbills, splendid with their double-decked bills and black and white plumage. They announce their approach from a distant tree by the beating of their wings which produces a humming sound like a tube train making its way through the tunnel to a London Underground station. They are usually seen in pairs and when the first hornbill leaves a tree its partner is only seconds behind. Close to our popular tree is the boundary fence. One of the fence posts is often the resting place for a long crested eagle. This majestic specimen has a blackish brown appearance, a high black crest and legs feathered brownish white. If the bird is not seen then we know it is around by its call: 'kee, ee, ee, ee'. This eagle feeds almost entirely on rodents and other agricultural pests and for this reason is a most beneficial bird.

One morning from my window I saw a blue monkey sitting on the same fence post. This proud male was about twenty-four inches in length; a rather large, stoutly built creature with a long thick tail. I have always been fond of monkeys and welcomed his presence by throwing a banana. Unfortunately he thought this was a different kind of missile and leapt away into the bush. I placed two bananas on the fence to entice it back, but this idea was not viewed with enthusiasm by the neighbours due to the damage monkeys cause to crops especially any fruit which is ripe for picking. If the monkey would eat just one fruit from a bunch or branch of guava, banana or mango, it might be forgiven. Unfortunately its habit is to take a bite from each fruit it finds and this destruction understandably cannot be tolerated by people who depend on their crops for both family food and as a source of income. Early one morning just as dawn was approaching, Charles took me into a nearby forest to see troops of monkeys searching for their breakfast. We tried to hide in the undergrowth by the side of their route through the tree tops. Being arboreal feeders they usually ignored the ripe fruit which had fallen to the forest floor. That morning we saw two family groups making their way from tree to tree a few yards from where we were standing. Small hands were plucking fruit, taking a bite before letting the remainder fall to waste below. Younger members of the family seemed more intent on play than feeding and had to be hurried along by adult females. The first troop enjoyed a hurried meal but the second family was not so fortunate. Local boys had discovered the arrival of the monkeys and were pursuing them with a shower of stones. Where you have man and animals competing for the same piece of land, unfortunately man usually wins. Rarely do we manage to live in harmony with the wildlife around us. We just have to think of the wild birds of countries like France and Italy, or the mammals to be found in our seas, to remember how some species are being slaughtered to extinction.

As the sun begins to set behind the mango tree I start to hear the sounds, and sense the smells, of an African night. Groundnuts roasting on a charcoal fire. The aromas coming from different types of firewood cooking pots of vegetables. Meat and fish being steamed in banana leaves. Local drinks made from roasted soya beans to stronger brews from bananas and sugar cane. Noises come from Eastern grey plantain eaters, paradise flycatchers or sunbirds finding their perching place for the night. The screech of bats setting out on their nightly feeding trips. A high pitched scream coming from small tree climbing frogs. The grass is alive with the chirping of crickets and grasshoppers. Excited children having their bath by splashing themselves from bowls of water. An African night is usually noisier than the peaceful daytime.

You have to experience evenings in Africa to realise how dark the world can appear. With all the artificial light which illuminates European countries the same blackness is not experienced. My college students found it hard to believe that British suburban streets were lit by lights so bright that we had no difficulty standing beneath to read a book or newspaper.

My first experience of an African night was in the 1960s when I completed my university years and decided to make a tour of schools for the disabled in Nigeria and Ghana. After my first hotel dinner in the northern Nigerian town of Kano, I agreed to join an American friend taking a walk into town. We moved a few yards along the road to find that it was not possible to see the ground beneath our feet. Fearing that we might be walking on snakes, we hastily retreated to the safety of the Bristol Lounge. Walking along the side of a road at night in Uganda is fraught with danger. I fear the cyclists who ride their bicycles without lights. A bicycle will suddenly appear out of the dark, on the left, centre or right of the road, hardly giving you time to leap to one side. I have found myself more than once tangled up with a cyclist and his machine, both accusing the other person of being in the wrong place.

After dark is not a time to be in my office. If I do work late I see by the light of my oil lamp bats swooping in, frogs hopping out and rats running around the room. I therefore lock the office door, say good night to Adam and Margaret, our cook, and walk a winding route home around the potholes on our local road. Once again I am reminded how really dark an African night can be, illuminated by little more than the fleeting glimpses of hundreds of fireflies. When I reach the main road I wait for the first minibus which can squeeze an extra passenger on to its already tightly packed seats and hope we safely reach our destination. Tomorrow I will be able to return to my little office, under the shade of the mango tree, for another day.

Chapter Two

The Mango Tree

Mangoes have always been my favourite fruit since childhood days growing up in the subtropical area of Northern Australia. During the mango picking season we used to enter a garden stealthily, on our way home from school, picking up any fallen fruit close to the gate, until we heard a banging on a window and saw a threatening face. We would then scatter and find a quiet place to divide our booty before making our faces, hands and clothes a running yellow mess of sticky juice. Although this pastime brought frequent visits to our outside bucket toilet, we were always tempted back the next day to gather more of the delicious fruit.

Living many years in Africa I now have different memories of the mango tree. With its spreading branches and dense foliage the tree makes an ideal shelter from both sun and rain. Under a mango tree is the favourite meeting place in towns and villages throughout Africa. A spot where ladies will sit and sell their home-grown produce, while gossiping about a neighbour's behaviour or condemning their own husband's indiscreet infidelity. Many of the ladies will have a baby on their back, tied in a colourful cloth. As soon as a baby wakes up and cries it is given a breast to satisfy its needs. Men will sit under a tree for hours talking, debating, arguing late into the night, until they have managed to solve all the problems of the world. However strange to say, the following day the same men are back under the same tree, trying to solve the same problems. The trees are also places where animals are tethered, bicycles repaired and men go to have their hair cut. I have seen many a school lesson taught under these useful trees.

The town of Tabora in central Tanzania is known for its roads lined with mango trees. I used to walk around in the heat of the day – hardly came out of the shade, walking from tree to tree. The same convenience was experienced during the wet season when one could keep fairly dry in a tropical downpour by keeping beneath the closely planted trees. Although this is a pleasant experience today, especially when the fruit is falling into our hands, providing a refreshing drink and a snack, it was for a far more sinister reason that these trees were originally grown. Last century Tabora was the main assembly point for the slave trade in this part of the world. These were the slaves captured by Arab traders or bought from local African chiefs. The selling of slaves to the Arabs was both a lucrative business for the many chiefs and also a useful way of disposing of their enemies. I do not know if the Arab traders were any more brutal than the European or American slave dealers but on both sides of the African continent countless thousands of men, women and children suffered cruelty and death for more than a hundred years.

Thinking of the slave trade in the New World I was surprised to read what I think is a little known fact. During the 1750s there were more white slaves than black slaves working in all the islands of the Caribbean except for the island of Nevis, where there were more black slaves than white. These European slaves went to work in the various plantations in the West Indies from prisons in the home country of the governing power occupying that island. The descendants of white slaves can still be seen today on some of the Caribbean islands. They tend to live in groups and are referred to by the main inhabitants of the island as 'the poor whites'.

Returning to the mango trees of Tabora, each tree in the town became a convenient shelter for collecting groups of slaves before they were marched off to Bagamoyo on the coast, a journey of six agonising months. The Tanzanian town of Tabora was situated not too far away from the boarders of present day Uganda, Zaire, Rwanda and Burundi. In the days of the slave trade, before the European Powers took part in their 'scramble for Africa', it was even easier for the trade to play off one tribe against another. Guns would be handed out to the chief who rounded up the most slaves. When we remember that present-day Tanzania has one hundred and twenty different tribes, each with its own language, then it is not difficult to see that much inter-tribal fighting took place at that time, which supplied a ready market for the Arabs.

A museum five miles south of Tabora shows something of the trade in slaves which went on during the early and middle years of the nineteenth century. This same building was the home of David

Livingstone and H. M. Stanley for six months in 1872 and was where Livingstone remained for a further six months after Stanley set out for the coast. After finding David Livingstone in Ujiji the previous year, Stanley rented this house from Arab traders, as a place where they could both rest before his planned walk of six months with Livingstone to the coast and a short boat trip to Zanzibar, where the British had a consulate. However, Stanley went off alone, Livingstone refusing to leave Africa where he was determined to remain until he had finished mapping more of the great lakes of Central Africa. David Livingstone was never to see Europe again. After his death two faithful porters, Susi and Chuma buried his heart under a tree, carrying out Livingstone's wish that his heart should remain in Africa. His two companions then wrapped his body and carried it from Central Africa to Bagamoyo, where it was later taken across to Zanzibar and finally to Britain where it could be buried 'with his own people'.

Susi and Chuma were later invited to England by a friend of Livingstone and they attended a service in Westminster Abbey. The Livingstone Museum in Tabora is a suitable place to keep alive the memory of this great man who endeavoured to help the different peoples of Africa. One of his greatest struggles was against the slave trade and its Arab dealers. He constantly battled with these men and must have been the biggest thorn in their flesh, but they respected him when they could so easily have killed this ardent adversary. The museum shows various implements and weapons used in the capture and confinement of slaves. Also maps, drawings and documents which showed how the trade was operated. Many valuable books, papers and newspaper articles of the period tracing Livingstone's years and many expeditions in Africa can be seen. Unfortunately the contents of most rooms have not been well looked after and yearly deterioration has taken place. Climatic conditions, the eating by insects and dry conditions are causing the disintegration of irreplaceable records. On my last visit to Livingstone's African house I was surprised to discover in the back yard an old iron cooking stove which had printed on the front, 'Made in Scotland 1854'. A piece of history, still in working order. I wonder who brought that to Africa?

Walking around Tabora, under the shade of the mango trees, I used to think of the horrors, the brutality and greed which existed at that time and the suffering of the captives. Heavy irons and chains not only shackled the ankles, joining slave to slave, but they were also linked neck to neck. If one slave faltered or fell then he was cut out of the irons with his remains being left at the side of the track. A mother was allowed to keep her baby or child so long as it did not impede the rate of travel. If the infant caused any inconvenience then it was bayoneted and left to die.

Unfortunately for the people of present-day Tanzania they were treated little better than slaves by the first European power which controlled their territory. Tanganyika, as the country was called before it joined with Zanzibar in the 1960s to become Tanzania, was a German colony, until the First World War. After the defeat of Germany the colonies were divided among the victorious European states. Living in a German colony, Tanganyikans did not have too many problems with their European masters, as long as they worked hard and caused no trouble. If a Tanganyikan labourer did prove to be lazy or troublesome in any way he was shot. The colonial authorities back in Germany were concerned at the cost of so many bullets being used. To cut down on possible wastage they issued a ruling that for every bullet fired, the man with the gun had to produce an ear cut from the person shot, to prove that it had been a successful killing. This rule had to be changed at a later date when it was discovered that Germans were cutting off both ears of their victim and claiming two bullets for the one death.

We wonder how one group of people could behave in such an inhuman way to a less fortunate group of people only a century ago, until we think of what has recently taken place as we approach the end of another century.

Then I am reminded of my visit to the killing fields of Cambodia just a few years ago when I was shown the mass graves where between four and five hundred people were thrown into each hole. At least one grave contained two thousand bodies. The never-to-be-forgotten tree where the heads of children were smashed before being cast into this pit which was reserved for youngsters. The piles of skulls and the ground littered with fragments of bone and scraps of clothing peering through the soil. Coming closer to my present home, I am reminded of the scenes of the recent tragedy of Rwanda, where more than a million people were callously murdered.

Fortunately in present day Tabora the only heaps to be seen in the town are the piles of mangoes in the market. The size of the fruit ranges from the tiny variety, about the size of a chicken's egg, to the king mango which would cover an adult hand. When I moved into my Tabora house I was delighted to see a huge mango tree close to each of the four corners of the building. Almost daily I would watch the flowers turning into fruit and then grow and colour. I waited for the day when I would be plucking my favourite fruit. I began to wonder how I would dispose of the thousands of mangoes which would soon be coming my way. Working as a volunteer I was always short of money. I began to think about setting up a stall in the market, selling off the surplus fruit and at last making some money. I then thought what would happen if I was reported to my organisation, would I be sent home in disgrace? I need not have worried; sorry to say, I had just one mango to eat from the whole crop and that one I found fallen and out of sight in a patch of long grass. The problem I discovered was that when I was out at work each day the local children used to come and raid my trees and must have carried away armfuls of fruit. Certainly more than I collected from the ground as a boy in far-off Queensland. Some evenings on arriving home I would be approached by a child or two wanting to sell to me some of my own fruit. As you can imagine I did not completely miss out on this seasonal treat but ended up helping to keep down the size of the mango mountains in the market.

Chapter Three
As Others See Us

Maps have fascinated me from about the age of nine when my father gave me my first wall map of the world and a small globe which I kept on my bedside table. My mother told me that France was coloured green and all those other green blotches around the world belonged to France. My father said that Britain controlled more territories and I could see the colour pink scattered all around the globe. These two colours interested me because one half of my family came from the green areas and the other half were of pink origin. From those early days my aim was to travel the world, a feeling which has remained with me.

Sitting in my office in Africa I can see some of my maps pinned to the mud brick walls. One evening after a severe storm, which brought water running down the walls, my maps became a soggy mess, draped over the shelves of books and files. Luckily they soon dried out the following day and suffered little permanent damage. One map shows our capital city, although a number of street names have now changed, which happens when a new government comes into power. What used to be Malcolm X Street might now be named Prince Charles Road, or the other way around depending on the politics of the new people in control. A second map covers the three main countries of East Africa. The largest is a new map of the world giving all the difficult-to-pronounce new countries which broke away from the old Soviet Union. When I am writing and trying to recall a word or wondering if accommodation is spelt with one m or two, I find my eyes glancing at the world above my bookcase and I begin to remember previous journeys or visits I plan to make. When my eyes focus on one country I think of the people I met there and friends made during my travels. Perhaps Brother John, one of my colleagues in Tanzania. Piera, my young friend and her parents in New Zealand. Wonderful Mother

Theresa in Calcutta. Auld Jock in Scotland, who had more hairs growing out of his ears than hair on his head. The boy in a Sepik River village in Papua New Guinea who asked me if England was larger than their nearest town of Wewak.

Travelling from one country to another I never cease to be amazed how differently people think and behave. On one tour I saw villagers in eastern Nigeria prostrating themselves at the foot of a tree presenting it with fresh daily offerings. The people in Britain who worship the sun as it rises above a ring of stones on Salisbury Plain. Those who sail out to sea and throw flowers into the water as prayers are being offered to a sea god off the coast of one of the Fijian islands. A small group of men going down on their knees in awe at the sight of a gold disk as it was uncovered in a temple in Malaysia. Hordes of people paying daily homage to fruit machines in gambling palaces in Las Vegas. I am sure all these groups think their practice or their way of worship is the correct one and I ask myself who is right and who is wrong and who am I to question their behaviour? We look upon another group of people as being strange but perhaps they look upon us as being even more peculiar.

Brother John in Tanzania often told me amusing stories. We shared an office where he had worked for more than ten years but he had lived in the same area for more than twenty years. He belonged to the Order of White Fathers and lived in a community on the edge of town. The father who led the group had a team of workmen who cared for both the house and extensive grounds. He was satisfied with the way the men worked but had an idea that when he was away perhaps the men relaxed and spent more of their day resting. Before he departed on his next tour he called all the workers together in the main room and told them that while he was away he expected them to work hard each day and that he was going to leave his eye behind to watch them. This senior father wore an artificial glass eye. He then took out this eye, placed it in full view on the table and stated that the eye would remain there the whole time he was away, watching the men to see if they worked hard. For the next few days the workers kept busy and would occasionally glance at the eye on the table to see if it was still watching. Later that week one man who had been wondering how to overcome the problem of the ever watching eye, called his friends together and told them he knew how the difficulty could be solved. He took off his hat, placed it on the table over the eye and explained that now they did not have to work hard because the eye could no longer see them.

Customs differ so much from country to country and even within the same country where you have a number of different tribes or regions. When sitting in a principal's office in Thailand I heard a knock on the door and when the person was told to enter I was amazed to see a lady member of staff go down on her knees to move across the room until she reached the principal's table. This was even more of a surprise because she was trying to carry a tray of refreshments, but this was their custom. In Bangladesh a newly arrived teacher from England was sent to Coventry during her second week, with no one speaking to her for many days, because she had been seen taking a biscuit from a plate with her left hand. In some countries the left hand is used for something other than touching food. In one country in southern Europe a lady does not put her handbag on a table in a cafe or restaurant unless she is looking for men friends. I often use sign language in my work and this can bring confusion when travelling because a sign which is quite acceptable in one country might be a gross insult in another. The 'F' position in one-handed finger spelling can be interpreted in ways other than a position in the alphabet for deaf people. This hand shape when shaken slightly from side to side means okay to Americans. In France it often means 'zero'. To the Japanese it means money, and when used by a Tunisian it states, 'I will kill you.'

When I go to a new country I try to observe and ask about local customs but at times I have made mistakes. Visiting a school for the disabled in Thailand I was approached by a boy of about seven years who proudly showed me a page from his exercise book. Following the habit I have used in other countries I gave a smile and a pat of encouragement on the head. I was quickly told by his teacher that in a Buddhist country you never touch a person on the top of the head, the holiest part of the body, as this action would upset and insult. Whereas the top of the head has to be treated with great respect the feet are the opposite, the unclean part of the body and to sit with the legs crossed and the toe pointed towards another person is the greatest insult to offer. When Lyndon Johnson was president of the United States of America he was invited to meet the King of Thailand, King Bhumiphol, in the Royal Palace, Bangkok. President Johnson was sitting opposite the king, legs crossed and the toe of his large

Texan boot moving backwards and forwards towards the king. A member of the American Embassy staff had a quiet word in the president's ear but Johnson's response was that these were 'old wives' tales' and continued with the insult. People in Thailand today still talk about rude President Johnson who insulted their king.

Taking my first lecture with a new course of students I always make the opening session a getting-to-know-you hour. We introduce ourselves and I welcome an exchange of questions. Three questions are always asked by students: 'Are you married?', 'Do you go to church?' and 'What is your tribe?' The easiest question to answer is about my tribe. I say that in England today people do not talk about belonging to a tribe but if I looked back in history I would come from the Iceni people. I would talk about our great Queen Boudicca and how she drove the Romans out of areas of the south-east of England nearly two thousand years ago. When I answer 'no' to the questions about being married and attending church my students find this difficult to understand. The majority of people in developing countries attend daily or weekly worship. I try to explain that in Western European countries the number of people who go to church once a week would be about five per cent. I then have to explain to my group why church attendance has declined over the last few decades. This reminds me of the occasion when I was attending a church service in the north of England and enjoyed listening to a preacher who came from Africa. Talking with this man after the service I was intrigued to hear him say that he had gone to England to try to convert the people there to Christianity. Very few men in Africa remain unmarried. My students usually wanted to know why I was still single. One student in Tanzania stated that he would like to have nine wives. He said he would send them all out to work in the fields and sit at home and watch the money come in. I was visiting a town in eastern Uganda and happened to meet one of my students. She invited me to visit the home of her sister who lived a short distance from town. We approached a building which I thought was a primary school because of the fifty or more children playing in the grounds. My student laughed at this idea, explaining it was the home of her sister whose husband had many wives and these were all his many children. Today in East African towns, the modern man, the city man, is having fewer children. More and more parents follow family planning ideas and aim for a smaller number of births. It is understood by many couples that in the modern world it has become more difficult to feed and to educate a large family of children.

An African man had recently been promoted to a higher government office and was shortly leaving for his first official visit to England. He told a friend that he was happy with meeting men at the various receptions which had been arranged, because men talk about similar things where ever they come from, but he was not sure about topics to discuss with English women. His friend said there would be no problem because women are the same in all countries wanting to talk about marriage and children. When this diplomat attended his first function in London he found himself seated between two ladies and remembered the advice given by his friend at home. He turned to the lady on his right and began the conversation by asking if she was married. This lady appeared friendly and answered 'No', but this new friendship quickly froze at his next question, when he asked her how many children she had. Not sure of his mistake he next turned to the lady on his left and thought it might be better to ask about children first. This lady informed him that she had four children but did not appreciate his second question, when he asked if she was married.

It is so easy to make mistakes in a foreign land and sometimes these can prove to be fatal. One European was killed in the market of Tabora, the reason being that he had taken photographs and not everyone wished to be filmed. During that same year a tourist from North America visited a village near Tabora and started taking pictures of some village girls. Men told him not to take photographs in their village. The foolish man continued and he did not leave that village alive. When attending an orientation course in Uganda the British High Commissioner told us to take no pictures outside the game parks.

When travelling in some countries I prefer to be accompanied by a local friend who understands both the language and customs of the area. This is also a big help when setting up a new home. In Kampala I went with Charles to the market to buy a plastic washing bowl. He gave the stall holder seven hundred shillings, the correct price. That same day an English friend made the same purchase by himself. He was not sure of the local money and was charged seven thousand shillings. One shopkeeper we met told us that he charged according to how the customer arrived at his shop. If he came on foot one price was charged. A person arriving on a bicycle would have to pay a higher price. Customers who approached in a car would be charged the largest amount. When I wanted to have a new suit made to measure, Charles would go by himself to ask all the questions. He would explain just what his 'father' wanted, have the price reduced as far as possible and have the material placed on one side. He would then collect me and we would appear together. I would show that I did not understand what was happening but Charles would insist that we bought at the price previously agreed to. We were always successful but could not return to the same shop for a second suit. Fortunately there were plenty of tailors in town.

Language problems can cause some embarrassing moments. Late one night I was returning to college when the guards on the gate all called out, "Simama." This was my first week in Tanzania and I thought the men were wishing me good night. I decided to answer in the same way and waved and said "simama" to each one. Next morning in class my retelling of this story brought howls of laughter from my students who explained that the guards were telling me to stop because they wanted to search me. I was told that the security men would not have been too surprised by my behaviour because they knew that all Europeans were a little mad. I always find it far easier to communicate in sign language when abroad than by a spoken language. Travelling for two hours across Bangkok by bus, from one school for the deaf to a similar school on the far side of the city, I sat in silence, not knowing the spoken language of Thailand. On the return trip I was accompanied by two deaf Thai friends and we enjoyed two hours of signed conversation.

Some African colleagues have told me of problems they have faced when studying in Europe. A Tanzanian friend was attending a degree course in Finland. His lady tutor explained one day that she was having a birthday party that evening and would be happy if Herman came to her flat for the celebration. He was not sure about a suitable gift to take, so asked one of his African friends who suggested flowers. Herman arrived at the flat, presented his bouquet, and wished the lady a happy birthday. Much to his surprise she gave him the news that the birthday party was being held for her dog.

I was walking along a street in London with a friend from Somalia when we stopped to admire a painting in a shop window. This picture showed the inside of a church but Ali, never having seen the interior of a church, thought the painting showed a hospital with the seats being hospital beds. Another friend took his first train journey in England and entered the compartment to find six businessmen reading their morning newspapers and making their journey to London. He remembered how polite English people had been in Africa so he went up to each man, said good morning and shook hands. Later it was explained that this was not the usual custom on the morning train. My Somali friend said that when he first arrived at one of the main London railway stations he was amazed to see white men sweeping up litter. Europeans in his own country sat in offices or were driven around in cars. His story reminded me of the time when I was spending a week in the house of one of my students in the Southern Highlands of Tanzania. One small village boy had asked his mother if Europeans had legs. Before I arrived he had seen Europeans driving in cars to a nearby tea plantation but never walking so he wondered if white people had feet and could move in the same way as Africans. Ali from Somalia told me that one day he travelled on a London bus. On the seat in front sat a small girl with her mother. This little girl turned around and gazed into Ali's face and suddenly said in a loud voice, "Mummy, why does that man have a black face?" Ali waited for the mother's answer, as I am sure other people on the bus did also. After a long silence the mother said, "Because he lives in a country near to the sun." I met an English couple who had been living in Uganda for about six months. The wife said that when she first arrived in Kampala all she could see around her were African people but now she just saw people.

We would have a more harmonious existence if we all had the same colour skin, perhaps a healthy-looking brown. This might not appeal to the makers of suntan lotions or to some fashion designers but it would help to lessen some of the racial abuse which is thrown about. Then again if we did all have brown skins I wonder if a different form of discrimination, superiority or stupidity might take its place as I discovered in Jamaica when the width of the nose was used to place a person on some kind of social scale. The broader the nose the lower down that ladder the individual slipped.

As a European I have encountered little personal abuse in Africa but the colour of my skin has brought about harassment in the Caribbean. Soon after moving into a house in St Vincent I took a walk into the capital of Kingstown. On my way I met two young teenagers who greeted me in a fairly harmless way with, "Hello, white man."

The two boys became a little apprehensive when I walked over to them and took out my (fortunately clean) pocket handkerchief, which had been biologically boiled white and said, "This handkerchief is white." I then placed it on my bare arm and said, "My skin is not white, I am not a white man, I am a brown man." The boys stared at me wondering what I would say next but I smiled, waved goodbye and walked away. I am sure that was a more suitable answer on my part than some European men I have heard who respond to "Hello, white man" with "Hello, black boy".

I used to experience racial abuse and a real feeling of enmity on the Caribbean island of Nevis. For one long year I lived on that unhappy island and received a daily outflow of abuse. This animosity came about due to my pale skin. Two favourite ways of greeting Europeans on Nevis was by referring to them as either 'white pigs' or 'white scum'. These vulgar comments were shouted out by all age groups both young and old. Words would often be accompanied by a fascist fist salute or by spitting on or near that person. The saddest incident I experienced on the island occurred when I was returning to my house one day for lunch. I approached a group of about twelve children of nursery school age sitting with their teacher in the shade of a large tree. They all sat in silence until I was a few yards away, then with one voice they chanted, "White pig, white pig, white pig." Amazed, I looked at their teacher but she kept her head well down. The whole event was so obviously instigated by the teacher and was not something which children of nursery school age would do by themselves. On another occasion I was walking along the same dirt track with my mother when we saw a small pick-up truck coming towards us. The driver's aim was to make us jump from the road into the ditch, which we did to avoid being mowed down. This was no easy task for my mother who was then approaching her eightieth birthday. As the vehicle regained the centre of the road the four men travelling in the back saluted with their raised fists and shouted the usual, "White pig, white pig, white pig," which continued until the truck was out of sight.

I wondered how relations between the Nevitians and Europeans had deteriorated to this level. When living in England I had more West Indian friends than when I lived in the West Indies. I worked in different Caribbean islands for three years before I was invited into a West Indian home. The arrival of Charles in St Vincent brought about a change. He came from Uganda to help me with the running of workshops for teachers in mainstream schools. Perhaps seeing this European with an African friend made people realise that my social life was not exclusively European-orientated by choice. How does the West Indian in the Caribbean look upon visitors from North America and Europe? The most common view is that a white skin means money. Some are wealthy and can be seen scattering money around as if it was their final day. Others have worked hard at home, saved for a year or more and decided to spend their earnings on two weeks in the sun instead of a holiday in their own country. Alternative choices might have been a change of car or a regular supply of drugs which is ruining the lives of so many people living in the Caribbean area today. Another common belief which I often hear expressed is that all Europeans have AIDS. This idea was stated not just by the elderly or voiced by the churches but seemed also to be in the minds of the younger age group. To have a close relationship with a white person meant that you were dead or soon would be. One West Indian friend asked if I thought he was a monkey. I was shocked by his question and asked him to explain his meaning. He next asked if I thought he was an ape. He was a beautiful person, attractive in appearance, with charming manners and personality, well educated and highly intelligent. I discovered that his question echoed a statement recently made by his grandparents who said that all Europeans thought Africans were monkeys.

Chapter Four
One World, One Day?

Sometimes when an afternoon is quiet and the children are busy with one of their craft activities, I will take my notebook and sit in the shade of our mango tree. This is the time of day when temperatures make any shelter from the sun most welcome. Perhaps I begin to write a letter to a friend in a far away place. Maybe to Violet or Eve at home in my village or to Terry in London. Often my attention is captured by a gaudily decorated butterfly, fluttering around to gain satisfaction from one of hundreds of flowers scattered about. Then I might hear the call and notice, another brown bird, and wish I had not left my bird spotters' book in the office. Bird watching might lead me on to thinking about my early mornings in a tent in the Okavango Swamps, Botswana, where I used to be woken each morning by the cackle, laugh, squawks chatter or whistle of more than a hundred different bird calls. I think my bird spotting list for Okavango amounted to one hundred and twenty-two species.

Perhaps my thoughts would go next to camp meals eaten in the swamps. These were as good as a five-star city hotel, complete with silver candlesticks on each table. Even when I am sitting at home in England my mind wandered abroad. I always remember a saying my father used to quote: "A knowledge of the world is the foundation of education and education is the foundation of life." I was first taken overseas by my parents when I was four years of age. Fifty years later I am still travelling. I have visited more than one hundred different countries in the world, but have not reached half the total number. So many lands and peoples to see but so little time available.

It still surprises me how legislation's modus operandi or custom of habit has treated different races in the same country in different ways. When Sir Robert Menzies was Prime Minister of Australia he participated in a number of meetings with leaders of Aboriginal groups, from the different Australian states in the capital of Canberra. During one break between sessions he invited delegates to enjoy some refreshments, including alcohol. The leader of the Queensland contingent told the Prime Minister that in their home state he would have been put into prison for such an invitation. That was the penalty for such an act in that part of Australia when a European offered an alcoholic drink to one of the original inhabitants of the country.

My father experienced a different drinking problem when working in South Africa in the late 1940s. He was employed as a civil engineer and his work took him around Cape Province, moving from project to project. One day my father was travelling to a different construction site with the head of a new building scheme. They went in a small pick-up truck with five African men sitting in the back. After a journey of about one hundred and fifty miles the driver suggested that a refreshment stop should be made at a cafeteria. When walking into the building with his colleague Father asked about snacks for the men in the back of the vehicle. He was soon told that they did not need refreshments. My father went to the counter and asked for six cups of tea and a plate of cakes. These he took outside to eat with the men in the truck. This behaviour was observed by people in the cafeteria, including the owner. On his return to the pay desk with the tray the manageress picked up one cup at a time and smashed each one on the floor stating, "We do not do that in South Africa."

Walking into the grounds of a five-star hotel in one East African capital city I noticed that security men were checking all bags and parcels. When I approached the gates, ready to be searched in the same way, I was waved through and my bag was not inspected. The people ahead of me were all African, mainly well-dressed businessmen, off to some hotel function or dinner appointment. My dress was not the smart suit and tie as worn by the other men but because I was European I was allowed to walk through the security check without being searched. I entered the hotel and asked to see the manager. The next few minutes saw a mainly one-sided discussion, with me expressing the view that if a security system was in operation, then all should be checked, regardless of race, and the manager adding just the two words, "Yes, sir."

People abroad find it difficult to understand the feelings of most British people towards animals. I once overheard a conversation between two ladies in my home village of Polegate. One was asking her friend if she had heard the news that Mrs Jones had just died. The answer she received was, "No, what will happen to her dog?" There was no mention of poor Mrs Jones. I remember two Englishmen in Zambia, who lost their jobs and had to leave the country because of a dog. They both worked at a teachers' college and had been invited to have dinner in the home of their Zambian head of department. When the two guests had eaten all they could of the main course, they placed their plates, containing the remains of the meal, on the floor for the dog to finish. Their department head took this as a personal insult to his hospitality and refused to work with them again. They both left the college and, having no other work in Zambia, had to leave the country. I was travelling through a village in northern China when I saw teenage boys catching wild birds. The following behaviour shocked me. Each bird was held in the hand and had its feathers slowly plucked off as the birds were struggling to escape. The boys looked upon this as a great game and could not understand my disgust at the cruelty.

It is also difficult for people to understand the European love of flowers. When I establish my college gardens in different countries I try to collect and grow plenty of flowers plus flowering trees and shrubs. My students used to ask why I grew flowers because we can't eat flowers. However, when end of term arrived and students wished to take individual and group photographs, my garden was the place they made for. When a young member of the college was killed, my garden flowers were again in demand. No use could be made of the cabbage leaves or carrot tops from the other gardens. When I take a new post abroad I know now never to take packets of flower or vegetable seeds from Britain. When I have tried this experiment overseas I have had only about ten per cent growing successfully. The packets of seeds available in Britain are produced for British growing conditions and will not usually flourish in a tropical climate. However, I have had success the opposite way around, finding that a number of 'tropical' plants grow happily in England, if they are given the necessary protection during the winter months.

Crime, punishment and death are viewed differently from country to country. An English teacher friend in Tanzania went home early from school one afternoon to find her front door ajar. On entering the house she saw a man helping himself to her possessions. This lady ran outside shouting, "Thief! Help! Thief." Neighbours came running, caught the robber and started to beat him with sticks and pelt him with stones. Jane wanted the man punished but did not want a killing. She now attempted to stop the beating until the police arrived. When the police officer looked at the thief his first comment was, "This man is still alive, why did you not kill him?"

In the same town a Danish nurse saw a crowd catch a bag snatcher outside her house. The usual beating and stone throwing took place and continued until the thief appeared to be dead. After a pause someone noticed that he was still alive. Dried grass was collected, piled on top of this unfortunate man, set alight and he was burnt to death. Three car thieves in Dar es Salaam were cornered by a crowd. They managed to leave the car and ran into a police station where they knew they would be safer than left outside with the mob. In many African towns you just have to shout "thief", point at someone and run in their direction and people will swarm after you to carry out the execution. That is one way people use to rid themselves of an enemy or a person they are heavily in debt to.

Last year I was home in England to arrange for the burial of my mother. In the funeral parlour I happened to mention that the last funeral I attended was far easier because we buried the body in the back garden. I was looked at in such a way by the lady writing down the arrangements that I could see she was about to pick up the telephone to instigate a police enquiry. I quickly explained that the funeral I was referring to took place in Africa. When a person dies in many parts of Africa it is not uncommon for two hundred or more relations, friends and neighbours to attend. People arrive the day before, sleep out around the house overnight and cook their meals on individual fires. The grave is often lined with bricks and once the coffin has been lowered a layer of bricks and cement covers the top.

I have heard some strange stories told about this morbid subject of death. In Malawi a British couple explained how they had received their regular food parcel from home. This particular package contained an item they did not recognise. Not sure if it was a gravy mix or a new type of flavouring they decided to add it to their next casserole. The following week a delayed letter arrived to say that the next food parcel would contain a packet of grandmother's ashes, which she wished to have scattered in Africa.

A tour guide in Denmark told us the story of an eight year old boy going off on a month's holiday to a farm. His parents were surprised when he arrived home again at the end of the first week. The mother said she thought he would have enjoyed farm life and asked why he came home early. The boy answered by saying he liked the farm but on the first night a chicken died. Next day they had chicken for dinner. The following day a sheep had died. That night the sheep was cooked for supper. Then Grandmother had died, so the boy ran home.

Two young men went from England to work in Papua New Guinea. The mother of one man was very worried because she had heard of people being killed and eaten in that country and pleaded with her son to be careful and to make sure he wrote home each week. In every letter she wrote the mother told the young man to beware of cannibals. The son became so tired of this that he asked his friend to write home to say sorry and to explain that Peter had been eaten by the natives. The mother, of course, believed this and it took a great deal of time for the aid organisation responsible for the project to investigate, discover the joke and to convince the poor mother that her son was alive and well. I was in Papua New Guinea during one of their regional elections. A disturbance took place in one highland village and four policemen from the nearest town were sent to calm the situation. These four men never returned; they were killed by villagers, placed in a cooking pot and made into a meal.

One college holiday a student invited me to stay in his village for a week. Four adults lived in the house but every night the mother would use five plates and serve five meals. When I asked my student friend who had the extra meal I was told that it was placed outside for his father. The father had been dead for over thirty years but every evening his plate was set on a table at the back of the house. I was assured that next morning the plate was always empty.

One of the most encouraging events of this final decade of the twentieth century has been the right which has been given to all people in South Africa to choose, through the ballot box, which party will govern their country. My early memories of South Africa sprang from tales my father told me when I was a young boy. He broke his contract to work in South Africa, and returned to England, disheartened by the way the majority of the population were treated by the governing few. My father became aware of apartheid during his first week. He was visited by a church minister and asked if he would like to attend church the following Sunday. Father arrived early and sat watching the congregation arrive. After some time he began to wonder where the African members were because sitting around him were all Europeans. He approached one of the church attendants to ask why were there no Africans in the church. He was given the answer, "Africans? We do not let Africans into our church." My father returned to his apartment never to return to church during his following nine months in that country. If he had remained longer in South Africa I think he would have ended up by being deported or even worse.

My first visit to South Africa was in 1988. By this time apartheid had started to die a slow death but I still saw lingering signs of the system. Walking through a park in the centre of Johannesburg I needed to visit a toilet. I noticed a 'gents' sign and entered the small building. On the inside I found four or five African men looking at me in a strange way. I did what I had to do then quickly walked out. Later I realised the mistake I had made. I had not taken careful notice of the symbol used for toilets. An outline of a black man on a white background was the toilet for Africans and a white man on a black background was for European men. I had not read my symbols correctly and had entered an African toilet. I am not sure if I could have been prosecuted for breaking that particular apartheid law. Another example of the discrimination between the races which existed in 1988 was to be seen at certain bus stops. In the national administrative capital of Pretoria I saw three seats which were labelled 'whites only'. Other labels I saw stated 'no blacks'.

In 1992 I took Charles from Uganda to South Africa for a month's holiday. I did wonder if there would be any difficulty for a European and an African travelling together and if any apartheid rules still existed. During our stay and touring in three different provinces we did not experience one problem. We used public transport, ate in restaurants, shared hotel bedrooms and were welcomed in all areas. I was amused by the reactions of some Africans to the presence of my travelling companion. One afternoon we were entertained in the home of the ex-mayor of one of the main cities. A kitchen maid saw her mistress handing a cup of tea and plate of cakes to Charles. She strongly expressed her disapproval of this situation, when the owner of the house returned to the kitchen. This was a new situation for the poor maid, used to a working life of black servants waiting on white people and not the other way around, as she had just seen. We experienced similar situations a number of times in South Africa.

Talking with an African teacher we asked why one African should resent another African being treated as an equal by Europeans. He explained that this was due to a confusion of thoughts which must go around in a person's head. On the one hand it was a new situation to try to understand after a lifetime of apartheid. Secondly there was a certain amount of jealousy involved that one African should rise to a higher level than they had managed to reach.

Before going to South Africa Charles and I visited Zimbabwe. One evening we were enjoying a meal together in a restaurant in Harare, when Charles commented on the fact that we had visited hotels, cinemas, parks and restaurants together in different towns in Zimbabwe but so far had not seen Europeans and Africans mixing together. The two races always seemed to be apart socially. My answer was that the racial groups had grown up separately, attending different schools, churches, social clubs and so on, and that it would take a generation of integration in schools and colleges and churches and clubs, before close interracial friendships developed. Later Charles put the same question to a number of Zimbabweans and received very similar answers.

The way people treat the disabled differs from family to family, community to community and from country to country. Local beliefs and customs sometimes cause people to look down on the disabled as inferior human beings. In some areas people believe that children are born disabled because their parents did something wrong. Husbands will drive a wife away from the home, giving her the blame for the deformity, saying that there had never been a crippled person in his family. I have never heard a father blame himself for the birth of a disabled child. Some parents think that the birth of a disabled baby is a punishment from the gods for some bad deeds they had committed. They may feel that the child was born defective to pay for some sins performed in an earlier life. In such cases parents may feel that to correct a deformity or to limit the child's suffering would go against the will of the gods. Parents can look upon the blind, deaf, mentally or physically disabled child with shame and hide the youngster away in a small room or a dark corner of the house. I have heard of cases where a disabled person has grown up in a house without neighbours ever knowing of his or her existence. Neighbours will often refuse to allow their children to go near a disabled child thinking that the blindness or deafness is contagious. In one college I had no female students in my class training to be teachers of the disabled. When I asked why so few female teachers came forward for special training I was told that women thought that if they worked with the disabled they would give birth to a child with a similar handicap. This surprised me. I could understand the village girl who had never attended school having these ideas but not educated teachers.

In some communities children with a mental illness are said to be possessed by a devil or evil spirits. Such children are often feared or locked up or beaten. Failure to understand that a child with a disability can usually be trained to lead a fairly independent life may lead to them being neglected or abandoned.

It has been known for a mother to dispose of her deformed baby from fear of her husband or local community. I was shown cases in India where parents had deliberately broken the limbs of their child so that it could gain sympathy and therefore money from begging. In Nigeria the head teacher of a school for the blind showed me children who had been blinded through ignorance. These children probably had a mild infection during their early years and had been taken to a local doctor who thought the best way to deal with the problem was to pull each eye from its socket.

One way in which more understanding is now being shown to disabled children is through the system of integrated schooling. All children whether able or disabled attend the same school. Integration takes place for the more practical subjects with academic lessons being taught in small groups by specialist teachers. This can work in most cases if you have teachers who have additional training in the special teaching methods which are required for children with learning difficulties.

In some countries the old, large, residential schools for the disabled have disappeared. In their place we find classes or units for children with special needs, attached to the neighbourhood school. I have written extensively about mainstream schooling for children with special needs in my book *An Introduction to Children With Special Needs for Teachers in Mainstream Schools*.

There is a saying which states:

> If a child lives with criticism,
> He learns to condemn.
> If he lives with tolerance,

He learns patience.
If a child lives with acceptance and friendship,
He learns to find love in the world.

Chapter Five
Tanzania – College Days

The British High Commissioner's wife ran down the steps of their official residence shouting, "Who stole the bottle of whisky from our drinks cabinet?"

She waved down the driver of the departing minibus, slid open the side door, held out her hand and with a thunderous look said, "Hand it over."

The party of newly arrived volunteers eyed each other for a few embarrassing seconds until the guilty one sheepishly produced a bottle from under his safari jacket. Fortunately I was sitting in a Land-Rover to the rear of the bus, with fingers crossed, in the hope her ladyship would not demand from me the return of a handful of pieces of toilet paper which I had borrowed from their bathroom. This commodity was not available in shops and markets throughout Tanzania in the early 1980s and was to be found only in the hands of the privileged few.

Preparations for two years of college life in Tanzania, where I was going to be a lecturer in Special Education, began in England about a month before our evening of theft at the High Commissioner's house. My job description indicated that I would head a department, which sounded grand, but unfortunately I was to be the one and only member of staff in that section. I would have ten already qualified and experienced teachers to train as teachers of the deaf. It would be my responsibility to present lectures in all ten areas of study which constituted this diploma course. Fortunately I had ten weeks free from work or travel to sit at home with my typewriter to plan my lecture notes for this daunting task which lay ahead of me. However, on arrival at the college some months later I found this hectic period of preparation was mainly time wasted, but that was to be one discovery among many others.

Close to our departure for Africa, an orientation course was arranged as an introduction to working in a Swahili speaking country. Three weeks were spent at a monk's retreat in Kent during the month of January. Some of us did not appreciate the spartan conditions encountered. It was true we were volunteers but we did not expect to sacrifice our health due to the lack of heating in austere working and living quarters. Language classes formed the major item of study. Our teacher was a man from Zanzibar, the island where the purest Swahili is said to be spoken. After three weeks of study, Saidi asked us to produce a sentence in his native tongue. My feeble offering of "Asanti sana, napenda Kiswahil" ("Thank you very much, I like Swahili") put me at the top of the class. As a course for teaching us a new language it was a failure. This was due to the theory that no English should be used during teaching. Instead we had to guess the meaning of a word or phrase from the context in which it had been presented. Far better if this introduction to the language had taken place after our arrival in Tanzania. We could have been housed with local families for at least those three weeks spent in England, and learnt Swahili from real life situations.

During this initial orientation course I first heard the term AIDS mentioned. On a freezing Saturday morning an elderly doctor travelled from London to give us what was called a health briefing. One man in our group asked the speaker if he would talk about AIDS, but he refused. Probably he knew little about this fairly new disease; unfortunately the doctor did not attempt to discover the necessary information and return another day with the facts. When asking my neighbour what this AIDS was, he informed me that it was a newly diagnosed, fatal disease, which had started to kill an ever increasing number of people, especially in Africa. We soon found out the devastation which this tragedy was to bring to all parts of the world.

We left the cold of England to arrive the same day in hot, humid, poor, but friendly Tanzania. A week was to be spent in Dar es Salaam – the name means 'haven of peace' – before our group was to scatter to a dozen or more locations throughout this large, mainly arid country. This first week brought us a number of speakers, who would try to help us to survive for two years in a developing country which had been taken into bankruptcy by a leader, who had admired, and tried unsuccessfully to follow, strict socialist objectives.

After an interval of twelve years I remember just two items from those seven days of enlightenment. Our group was composed mainly of teachers going into secondary schools and colleges. The minister of education came to tell us to try our 'level best' to teach English to our students. Tanzania was being handicapped by having Swahili as its national language, so the minister stated. Textbooks at the secondary and higher levels of education were printed in English, as were most forms of trade and communications. We were urged to promote English whenever we had the opportunity.

The second speaker I remembered was a man who appeared one night with a large, sealed plastic bucket. The topic for the evening was 'Reptiles of Tanzania'. All eyes were on the container as the lid was carefully prised off and to our amazement he plunged his hand into the bucket. After a few swift actions out came the hand clutching a highly decorative five feet of wriggling snake. We were shown how to recognise this captivating creature and advised on what action to take if we did receive a bite. As soon as the first snake was returned to the bucket a different variety was displayed in all its glory. This performance continued until a larger snake appeared but this time our presenter did not remain behind his table. He approached the group trying to loop the snake around our necks. The first people he approached quickly scattered to the back of the room. My reasoning was that this breed was harmless, otherwise he would not be offering this reptile for us to hold. Therefore, I let him drape it around my neck and shoulders and to hold its neck in one of my hands and tail in the other. This mock bravery produced undeserved admiration from my colleagues and numerous photographs.

A chance meeting with the head of the British Council in Tanzania gave me unexpected news of an old friend from my university days in Manchester. Rodwell Munyenyenbe left his home in Malawi in 1965 to travel to England to train as a teacher of the deaf. At that time there was no school for the deaf in his home country. The Malawi government had chosen this young headmaster to open their first school for deaf children when he had gained his qualifications in education and audiology. We became close friends during those years, with Rodwell often spending his holidays in my home. After successfully completing his studies he returned to Malawi and received the news that the government would not recognise his two British qualifications. During his stay in England, two Europeans had been

42

invited to Malawi to open the country's first school for the deaf, so Rodwell was no longer needed.

In frustration and disgust my friend abandoned the idea of working in special education and returned to his home area in the north and resumed teaching at his old school. Eighteen months later he was invited to represent his region in a one-party national election. Rodwell won and became a member of parliament. He rose rapidly through the party ranks and within two years was the minister of education. Later he became a cabinet minister with the portfolios of trade and communications. Rodwell represented Malawi twice at Commonwealth Heads of State Conferences. Although he was a leading member of Banda's government, he never personally believed in many of the policies of Hastings Banda, but in order to stay alive he had to keep his own counsel. In 1977 Rodwell invited me to visit Malawi, saying that as a government minister he would be able to escort me to any place I wanted to see, using his ministerial car. Unfortunately I had planned a visit to Malaysia that summer so we decided to postpone my Malawi trip until the following year. I haven't seen or heard from him since.

When the British Council man in Dar es Salaam told me that he used to be head of the British Council in Malawi, I asked if he had ever heard of Rodwell Munyenyenbe. He said that one of Rodwell's sons and his own boy were the best of friends and he frequently visited their house in the capital. To the best of his knowledge Rodwell was still alive and had not been killed in some of the fake car accidents which Banda arranged for his ministers when they failed to praise and support their 'president for life'. However, early one morning there was a knock on Rodwell's door and he was taken away to spend the rest of his working years back in his home village in the north, working on his shamba (land around a house used for growing fruit and vegetables). Now that Malawi is free from Bandaism, I hope to return to the country for a reunion with a good friend and a fine man.

Our orientation week in Dar, as most people came to call Dar es Salaam, was completed and arrangements were made for us to travel to regions near and far to join our projects. My college was situated in the dry centre of Tanzania, a journey by train which took between twenty-four and thirty-six hours, but had been known to take twice that long. There were four possible ways of reaching Tabora from the coast. Flying, but when booking a flight it was never known if Tabora Airport would be open on the day of travel. I experienced the airport closed for three months because the fire engine was not working. On one famous occasion an aeroplane could not land because the runway lights had been switched off. Ground staff had chosen that time to make a pot of tea and had used the socket, which operated the runway lights, to boil their kettle. There was a road which gave a second choice of travel but this two day, dry, dusty land journey was not possible at all times of year due to adverse weather conditions. Early travellers to East Africa used to walk for six months to reach Tabora but that does not suit visitors today. The route most people choose is by train.

One friend in Tabora was going home to India to attend his son's wedding. Due to all the hazards of travelling on local transport he made plans to go all three different ways. He booked tickets for himself and his wife to fly to Dar es Salaam; bought two first-class sleeper tickets on the train; and finally, just to make sure, he had a car and a driver standing by to go by road if both air and train routes failed to operate. He succeeded in his first choice and flew to the coast and arrived in time for the connecting flight which took them both to India to enjoy the wedding.

Large railway stations have always fascinated me and visits to Dar station did not fail to excite in the same way. People may spend many days walking, taking a series of buses or travelling along the coast by boat, before they reach the capital. This often leads to a wait of a few more days before their train arrives or before they can complete the complicated task of purchasing a ticket for their journey. Whenever I arrived at Dar railway station I found it difficult to walk anywhere between the main entrance way and departure gate for my platform. The whole ground area would be taken over by people sleeping or sitting patiently waiting for news of the expected arrival of their train. Food would be eaten on the spot, babies fed and changed, new friendships established and one eye kept open for possible snatch thieves. The arrival of a train might bring friends and relations; a body for burial; a prospective bride for her betrothal; soldiers for manoeuvres; students for training or traders for business. A departing train could be a major event in someone's life resulting in a first meeting or a reunion, a new term at school or college for the student, appointments at hospitals, orders to be placed by businessmen or holiday trips by tourists.

As the seemingly ancient locomotive trundled through the outer suburbs and following villages, children would run close to the track to wave passengers on their way. This great excitement shown by both travellers and onlookers was because it was not every hour a train would pass that way, as is usual in my home town in England. During my working years in Tanzania we had two trains a week on that main line. The only link between the Indian Ocean and Lake Tanganyika is the railway. So far, no road crosses Tanzania from east to west. The vital link between Dar es Salaam and Kigoma was established during the final years of the nineteenth century by German engineers. In fact their master plan was to link their colony of present day Namibia, along the Caprivi Strip which the Germans wanted to extend eastwards, until it met up with their colony in East Africa. One railway line linking the two oceans, Atlantic and Indian, and the two coasts of Africa. When travelling that same route through Tanzania today it seems that few improvements have taken place during the one hundred years of the track's existence. Trains travel at two speeds, slow and stop. We used to consider ourselves most fortunate if we completed our journey without the engine or some other essential part breaking down at least once. The longest I had to sit at the side of the track, in some remote area, waiting for repairs to be completed, was twelve hours. This was without any kind of refreshments being available on or off the train.

One February morning, twelve years ago, a first-class compartment had been booked for two English ladies, travelling from Dar to Dadoma. These ladies were volunteers going to be new teachers at one of the secondary schools in that town. I shared the next sleeper, also for two, with a student going with me to Tabora, a journey of a further twelve hours to the west The four of us from neighbouring compartments shared our food, conversation and a pack of playing cards, to help us to pass the time.

Our train stopped at most stations, giving us a chance to observe local life. An army of food and craft sellers would always swarm around each carriage trying to persuade us to buy from them and no one else. It was interesting to see that people from one area would usually specialise in one type of handicraft. At one station it might be hand carved walking sticks. The next village might offer baskets for sale. At a third station perhaps mat or stool makers would be offering their wares. If you wanted a walking stick and decided to wait until the next stop to compare price and workmanship you would be too late, because the next station might be the village where drums were made and not one walking stick would be seen for the rest of the journey. I found that craft goods being sold at the various railway stations were well produced and offered for sale at a lower price than could be seen in markets, shops, and craft centres, or than was offered by individual traders in the towns.

Food being sold remained very much the same from station to station. Ladies and children carried on their heads a tray or basket which might contain bananas, hard-boiled eggs, oranges, roasted maize cobs, small slivers of roasted meat or pancakes. There was of course much competition among the food vendors to make sure we bought from their basket. Running, shouting, pushing and sometimes fighting broke out, then police using long canes chased the boys away. Young men would clamber up steps on to the train. These were the ones we had to watch carefully in case they took away from the train more than they entered with. Usually this was a quick dash because the village stops were just for a minute or two. If I ever bought a cold drink I would almost choke gulping it down knowing the boy wanted the bottle before the train departed. Some passengers unkindly took delight in holding on to the bottle for as long as possible and when throwing it back from the moving train, would aim for some hard object, so as to smash the glass. The larger towns would provide a more leisurely pause with time to walk the length of the platform, exercise one's legs and to select a snack and drink without any great hurry. The stone-built stations in the larger towns were still the same buildings constructed by the Germans a hundred years ago.

The journey was long and hot and became more dry and dusty the closer we came to the centre of Tanzania. We experienced no real problems until evening approached. The railway crew told us to keep windows firmly closed until the following morning and not to unlock our compartment door, even if someone called out that he wanted to check our tickets. In the compartment I shared we continued with our cards and talk until the sleeping car attendant came along with the linen to make our beds. Occasionally I would hear someone running along the roof above me and my companion would say it was robbers but would reassure me that we were safe with doors and windows locked.

At about three o'clock the next morning I heard frantic shouts – "Roy, Roy, Roy! Help, Roy!" – coming from the next compartment. One of the girls had been woken from her sleep to find a man standing at the side of her bed. She caught the intruder in the act of lifting one of her bags out through the open window. The mistake the ladies had made was to go to bed with the window half open, thinking that because the train was moving no one could possibly enter their room from the outside. Two men had boarded the slowly moving train and climbed on to the roof. They had found the compartment with the open window. One man stayed on the roof while his friend lowered himself through the opening. The thief had then selected one bag and handed it to his partner above. It was when he was about to take the second bag that my friend was disturbed and discovered what was happening. Her screams sent the second bag, followed by the thief, hurtling through the now fully open window. Our train was travelling slowly, at little more than a walking pace, so it was an easy task for the robbers to escape with the stolen goods. My fellow volunteer lost a number of electrical gadgets, camera and £150 in cash, but what distressed her most of all was the loss of all her school teaching books, which could not be replaced in Tanzania.

This same young lady had further problems during her two years in the country. Later that year she was flying back to her project when the aeroplane crashed killing four passengers, all soldiers. She was injured but not seriously. After this fatal accident she used to say that never again would she fear flying because you are never caught in two air crashes in one lifetime. Not long after this her boyfriend was put into prison for killing a man in a road accident. I am sure she never forgot her two years in Africa.

After sad goodbyes and tearful waves to my two friends at Dadoma railway station, the train moved on its way to the next main station and depot, half a day's journey away, heading for Tabora. Trains stop at Dadoma for forty-five to seventy-five minutes, to refuel, have a change of crew and to allow for the movement of passengers. On one of my journeys west this long stop became a mere twenty minutes halt. Wilfred, one of my teachers in training, offered to show me some of the new government buildings, which it was hoped would turn Dadoma into the new capital city. After a hurried look around the new but dust-laden streets, Wilfred asked if I would like to enter a restaurant for a meal. I was anxious about our waiting train so decided to decline the offer and instead bought a loaf of bread. Walking back to the station we heard the alarming departure whistle. Our walk turned into a run and fears grew that we would miss the train. As we approached the station, gasping for breath, the train was moving away gathering pace with every passing second. Wilfred shouted out, "Mr Roy, jump on." We both tried to jump, Wilfred succeeded, but I fell back on to the track. Heads leaned out of windows urging me to drop the bread and try to jump again. Not wanting to wait three more days for the next train, I made a desperate leap, clutching a handle at the side of a door, with one foot on the step and the loaf of bread still in the other hand. A carriage door opened and friendly hands pulled me in. I took a slow walk, with faltering steps, through the train, receiving congratulations from some fellow passengers, until I came to my second-class compartment, shared by six men. Wilfred did not know whether I was on board and when I entered and sat down, we just shook hands for a countless number of times and laughed for some minutes. Our travelling companions could not understand what brought about this sudden outburst of joy. Wilfred told me later that his greatest fear had been the thought of returning to college to report that he had lost his tutor in Dadoma. After my safe arrival aboard the train, we shared my damaged, but rescued, loaf of bread.

At last, after an eventful journey of over thirty hours we reached the town of Tabora. I wondered how I would manage to transport my three pieces of luggage, from train to college, without losing any items. So many pairs of hands reached out to help, but who could I trust? Fortunately my travelling companion suggested I look after all our luggage while he went looking for transport. Before long, with the help of a porter, we moved our cases and bags on to a waiting handcart parked close to the station entrance. With cart and carrier, myself and student friend on either side of this rickety, home-made contraption, to stop items of luggage falling off, we made our way, in jerks and jolts, over dirt roads to the college, which was reached in under thirty minutes.

Tabora Teachers' Training College was a centre for over five hundred students taking their initial training course to become qualified, grade two teachers. A small number of the student population were well-qualified, experienced teachers, who had decided to return to college for two years to take a diploma in Special Education. This was my area of work. I soon met the principal, who greeted me with great enthusiasm. He told me not to think about coming into college to give lectures for a few weeks but to take all the time I needed to settle into my house, get to know my colleagues in the Special Education Department, meet my students and to generally familiarise myself with Tabora. This was not my idea at all as I was keen to begin my teaching programme, but I thanked him for his warm welcome. I was then escorted to my house.

Tabora College had six well-constructed brick built staff bungalows, completed about twenty-five years before my arrival. Unfortunately no maintenance or repairs had been carried out in all that time, as far as I could ascertain, not even a new coat of paint. The building consisted of three bedrooms, two bathrooms, large through lounge, a kitchen and an outside toilet. I never saw the inside of that outside toilet due to the high grass and probable snakes surrounding the place. This was a large home for one person, which made me feel guilty when I saw as many as ten adults and children living in each of the other houses. The bungalow was spacious but furniture and fittings were sparse. Contents amounted to: two iron beds; one and a half mattresses; large dining room table; the frames of three armchairs and an electric cooker, which never worked once during my two years in the house. The kitchen also contained a sink and some broken cupboards which housed many large, dead cockroaches. One of the two inside toilets worked. As soon as I turned on the water supply I discovered that the bath flooded the house every day. No plumber was ever able to solve that problem. Before long I collected four dining room chairs from college, plus a coffee table which I was told was surplus to the needs of the college staff room. The first weekend I cut up the half mattress to make seating for my armchairs. British friends in Tabora gave me an electric hot plate for cooking. I bought bedlinen, a mosquito net and a few other small household items. Fairly soon I began to feel almost at home.

Next day when our friendly principal came to the house I managed to persuade him to take me to meet other staff members in the Special Education Department. Remembering my job description, which stated that I would be the one and only member of that department training teachers of the deaf, and thinking of my three months of lecture preparations, I was rather surprised to find that I was one of a team of five lecturers. My four colleagues were all experienced teachers in the education of the deaf, having received their training overseas. My organisation had certainly not carried out their homework when vetting this job placement. College staff did wonder why I had arrived because they were already overstaffed with four lecturers to ten students and now a fifth person had arrived. However, I was made welcome and asked which two of the ten subjects I would like to teach. I thought this was kind, allowing the new man to take first choice; so when they persisted with their offer I chose history of special education and psychology as my subjects. This gave me about one day per week of lectures. I did not travel half way around the world to work one day in seven. Fortunately I managed to improve the situation by helping with lectures in the departments for the training of teachers going to work with the mentally retarded and the physically disabled.

My students, nine men and one woman, were a joy to teach: Assay, Castory, Constantine, Egata, Emanuel, Grace, Herman, Hokororo, Jonas and Wilbroad. All were training to become teachers of the deaf. Seven had been head teachers before joining this special course. Ages ranged from twenty-nine years to forty-six years. This was the first time I had taught students older than myself. They came from as far as the distant borders of Tanzania, from Bukoba in the north, close to Uganda, to Lindi in the south, near to Mozambique.

In some ways my students were too well behaved. They would not ask a question during my lectures, debate a point I had made, or discuss the facts presented to them. The reason for this was that they had been so conditioned to sitting and accepting everything their teachers said, without question, that no discussion ever took place. This had been their training from joining their first infant class, through primary and secondary schools and on to college education. I tried different ways of producing questions from the group but usually failed. It seemed that having their first European teacher, lecturer, further compounded the situation, confident that I knew all the facts. One tactic I tried was to give false information, obviously so wrong they would have to question my statement, but that also failed. An example was when I returned from a holiday in England I mentioned that I had visited a new school where dogs and cats were being taught to read. The result of this statement was the comment from one of the men who expressed the opinion, "Ah, England is a wonderful country, now they are even teaching animals to read. We will never reach that stage here in Tanzania, of teaching cats and dogs to read." However, I did not give up and as time went on I did achieve discussion as a part of my lectures.

Some of my fellow tutors did experience problems in running their programmes. Perhaps assignments were not handed in on time, students failed to attend lectures. or showed lack of respect to staff. I am not wishing to write a thesis at this stage on how to train teachers but will mention how I solved some of these difficulties. When I gave my weekly assignment I expected it to be returned within the seven days. It would not be accepted if it arrived a day late. The work would then be marked and returned at the next individual weekly tutorial. Students accepted this routine. A problem with some members of staff was that they would keep students' work unmarked for a long period, so there was not the same incentive for students to present work on time. When marking written work I would use a pencil to show wrong information or mistakes in spelling or grammar. These problems would be explained during individual tutorials and if the student wished he could erase my comments which were there not to find fault but to give guidance. My final mark and comments were always written in ink. I have so often seen teachers in both schools and colleges ruin a student's tidy page by careless marking, usually in red ink. Students were missing lectures for a variety of reasons: a visit to the doctor, dentist or hospital; they had to go to the bank or post office to collect money; a journey to the bus or railway station to meet a friend or relation; the need to visit a shop to buy a pen or exercise book. I started to keep an attendance register for my lectures and explained that if a student gained less than seventy-five per cent attendance during the course he would not receive his diploma. I usually achieved a one hundred per cent attendance. It was important to be truthful when a question was asked. If I did not know the answer I would say so and try to find the required information to give at my next session. Always respect your students if you wish them to respect you. Do not make a student lose face in front of his fellow students. This is so important to people in a developing country.

The students were always clean and tidy in their dress. Unfortunately many Europeans seen in the streets of Dar es Salaam, Kampala, and the main towns of Africa, dressed in the opposite way, presenting a sorry picture. I remember the director of our organisation telling groups attending for orientation, "Do not dress like slobs when overseas." It has been my experience that the untidy adults on African city streets are the Europeans. At college or in the town, I never wore shorts, T-shirt or sandals. I considered that to be house and garden or beachwear. Shorts in Africa are usually the dress of schoolboys or old men. Wearing unsuitable clothing for lectures is not the way to gain the respect of your students or colleagues. This reminds me of a new British governor who arrived at one of the Pacific Islands to take up his three year appointment. He stepped from the ship, to be greeted by the waiting crowds, dressed as a tourist and not in his official uniform and plumes of glory. He gained no respect from the local population and did not last long in this new position.

Near to the end of this diploma course one of my students said that the group had been pleased to have had a European tutor and not a Tanzanian. All heads nodded in agreement. When I asked him to explain, the reason given was that Europeans did not concern themselves with which tribe the student came from. Tanzanian staff gave high marks or grades to students from their own tribe or another tribe they favoured. I always felt that we should look upon our work as a partnership in which we were both doing a job. The tutor was working hard to train the students and the students were working hard to receive and to try to understand the training given.

As time went on I gradually felt more settled and comfortable in my college house. One thing which did disturb me was the fact that I had no curtains. It would be dark by seven o'clock every evening. I would sit in one of my easy chairs and see pairs of human eyes watching me through the windows, trying to see what this strange mzungu (white man) was doing in the house. I found a shop in town which had a large quantity of attractive curtain material, showing different African designs in black and white. The amount I bought was sufficient to cover ten windows, two long curtains for the glass doors, a cloth for both dining room and coffee tables, cushions for my three easy chairs and plenty remaining for a set of table napkins. All these creations I produced myself, hand sewing each item. First to be finished were curtains, which made me feel a little more secure at night but did not solve my security problems.

One evening there was a knock and when I opened my front door a large soldier, of the Idi Amin type, strode in wearing a black cloak to cover his uniform. He proceeded to sit in one of my armchairs and invited me to join him. His first question was to ask if I was frightened of him. When he heard that I was not he informed me that all Europeans were afraid of the military. I wondered what he wanted from me and was keen to be rid of him as soon as possible. He asked if I would give him my camera. When I explained that I needed the camera for my work but when I visited England at the end of the year I would return with one for him, he seemed satisfied and soon departed. Fortunately this man was later posted to another region so I did not experience another visit. The following week I opened the door to another caller and a drunk walked in. After a physical struggle to push him out, I decided not to open the door again at night.

When visitors arrive at a house they usually call out "Hodi", which means "Anyone at home, may I come in?" The answer to this is always "Karibu" ("Yes, you are welcome") before you even know who has arrived. This worked well in the villages but not so well in the towns, where robberies were frequent. I needed to find a safe way for my students to visit me during the evening hours. They would often come late afternoon after lectures, to enjoy tea and biscuits, but when it was dark it was not possible to see who was outside. The shout of "Hodi, Mr Roy" was not considered safe because it would not be difficult for a stranger to find out my name and soon have the door opened. My students suggested the idea of following "Hodi" with their name and home town or village. Now the call became, for example, "Hodi, Mr Roy, it is your student Herman, from Bukoba." Fortunately this system worked.

A Danish friend, working for a large aid organisation, thought my college house was far from secure. He told me one day that if a robber had the wish he could be inside the house within thirty seconds. My friend kindly had iron bars placed over all windows and doors, which made me feel safer, until he said, "Now it will take a thief at least one whole minute to be inside your house."

The same man often had to be away from Tabora travelling long distances to other projects. This meant having to leave his wife and two young sons at home alone. Before every safari trip he would place all his spare money in a box, in a cupboard, and tell his wife that if robbers came looking for valuables, to show them the cash box and hope they would leave satisfied. One neighbour who tried to argue with a group of armed thieves was shot in both legs, then had his money stolen. Friends from Finland, living five minutes drive from my house, kept five fierce Dobermanns in the hope these dogs would give them twenty-four-hour protection.

The unwanted visitors I did find in the house after the fitting of security bars were not of a human kind. These were rats and snakes! I discovered the rats entered through the broken, disused toilet. That problem was overcome by stuffing the toilet basin with chicken wire. One afternoon a female teacher from the local high school visited me for about an hour. After her departure I went to move the armchair to its usual place, when I spotted a brown snake asleep behind it. If the creature had been uncoiled it would have stretched to about five feet. I hastily disposed of the snake, not taking any risks in case it was poisonous. It was easy to keep snakes out of the house. I just had to keep the outside doors closed.

Not long after I left Tabora, my house was taken over by the college matron and her family. Friends wrote to tell me that a black mamba had entered the same sitting room and bitten one of the children. A bite from this deadly snake is usually fatal, but fortunately the matron had the necessary know-how and medicines at home and her daughter recovered.

Security outside the college grounds could also be a cause for concern. One evening around 8.30 p.m. I walked back to college after visiting an English volunteer friend who lived the other side of town. As I entered the college gates I was met by Sam, my head of department. He asked if I had walked from town to college. Sam quickly explained how dangerous that was and not to make the mistake a second time. He went on to recall what had happened to him a few weeks before, when he had returned to college on foot. Some men stopped him, stole his watch and all clothing, plus shoes, and left him with just his underpants to continue his walk home. When I heard this news I said that in future when returning after dark I would use my bicycle. Again Sam said no. He explained that robbers hid in the bushes at either side of the road, holding a thin piece of wire. When the cyclist approached the wire was raised to neck level, off the bicycle the rider would fall and the thieves would have the machine plus all the poor man's clothes and other valuables. I had many overseas friends living around Tabora Town and would be out for afternoon tea two or three times every week. After Sam's warning I would watch for the sun starting to set, make my quick farewells and frantically ride the sandy, potted tracks to reach the relative safety of the college gates, before it was really dark.

At times even motorised transport had its dangers. The eighteen year old daughter of one of my college neighbours returned home one evening by taxi. She disagreed with the fare the driver wanted to charge, an argument took place and she was hit in the stomach. She died two days later from her injuries.

One morning weird sounds of chanting brought me out of my first floor office. From the balcony I saw twenty men jogging in pairs, along the road below. Their dress and the weapons they carried startled me. Their bodies were decorated with animal skins and feathers and they carried spears, bows and arrows. Their repetitious slogans, and the purpose of this display were a puzzle to me until my colleague, Brother John, explained. This was a vigilante group which frequently patrolled the district warning offenders of the punishment they would receive if caught taking part in any illegal acts. Apparently the police gave these vigilante groups the freedom to carry out reprisals in the traditional way.

The arrival of a bank cheque was never a pleasure for me in Tabora. It would mean a struggle, almost a fight, for hours at the bank before I saw any money. Walking into the bank you would be met by an unruly mob each waving a cheque and passbook in one hand, trying to force their arm through the crowd, maybe as many as six deep, to reach the hand of a counter clerk. People would be pushing and shoving, trying to climb over each other – at times fists would fly. Complete chaos, which had to be seen to be believed. I could not face this melee by myself and used to go with a friend from college. He would gradually fight his way to the counter clerk with my cheque and passbook. We knew it would take about two hours to process so would return later to wait for my name to be called from a different part of the bank and the money handed over.

The most frightening and dangerous period I faced in Tabora was the time when President Nyerere decided to change all the banknotes to a new design. Instead of placing a notice in each bank in Tanzania, with such words as 'The current family of banknotes will continue to be legal tender and will gradually be withdrawn from circulation', he announced one weekend over the radio that people had until the Friday of that week to change their currency. If old notes were not changed for new during that five-day period they would no longer be valid.

The population panicked. Four people were killed on their way to the bank in Tabora the first morning. Towns being far apart meant that some people had a walk of fifty miles or more to change their money. Money in the villages was usually buried somewhere in or around the hut. This had to be dug up and carried to the nearest town with a bank. People were being robbed on their walk to the town. Crowds formed outside the Tabora bank some hours before opening time. Some of those same people would still be waiting to change their money at the end of the afternoon when the bank closed. I was advised not to leave college grounds for the whole of that week. The first afternoon I was invited by fellow members of staff to accompany them to the hospital mortuary to view the first four bodies to arrive, but quickly declined the offer. By the end of that traumatic week eighteen people had been robbed and killed in and around Tabora trying to reach the bank to change their money. I do not know how many hundreds of people died in the same way that week throughout Tanzania, as the result of the president's decision to have a rapid change of currency.

My college house was built close to the main student dormitories, women to the front and men to the left of my bungalow. Each dormitory housed over two hundred students, living on three floors. A college rule stated that men were not allowed to enter the women's residence at any time of day. However, men did break the rule; some by invitation, others by stealth. Every few weeks I would be disturbed from my evening reading or writing by ululations coming from the women's dormitory block. One female would start to wail or scream and this call would be taken up by every other lady in the building. This bedlam meant one thing: a man had been seen inside the residence. Within a very short time the neighbouring men's dormitory would erupt with all inhabitants charging to the women's building, picking up any weapon they could find on the way, to attack the intruder. If the interloper was caught, as he often was, he would be beaten to death. I was never sure what happened to the body – whether men students took it to the police station or the police collected it. One evening I heard the usual noise coming from the women's block, which indicated a man had been seen inside their residence, soon followed by the charge of men students. The intruder was caught and beating continued until someone noticed that he was a member of staff, who had been carrying out some extracurricular activity which broke the college rules. Punishment stopped and the lecturer was lucky to have escaped with his life.

Sitting in my house with some of my students one afternoon we heard a great commotion all around the bungalow. I thought it was a riot but we discovered that the majority of the college student population was trying to catch a member of the cat family, about twice the size of a domestic cat. My flowerbeds suffered but fortunately the animal escaped. Why were the students so keen to catch this wild cat, I asked? The answer was to cook, to supplement their meagre diet.

Food or the shortage of food was an ongoing problem students had to suffer. Seven days a week, twice each day, students were fed ugali – a thick porridge – and red beans, which took three hours of boiling before they were edible. Never was a piece of meat, fish, fruit or vegetable provided. As a result their health deteriorated. College work also suffered because students did not receive a diet which was conducive to lengthy and serious study. Towards the end of my first year at college I was asked one morning if my house had been raided by the police during the night. I had not had that experience but all other staff houses had been searched by the police during the early hours. A number of items were discovered, from large sums of money to thirty bottles of whisky under one bed. It had been found out that sufficient money had been received by senior members of college staff to provide students with a balanced diet. The money was alleged to have been stolen by six senior members of staff, plus one trader in town who had provided false receipts. The principal and vice principal were among staff charged. Our bursar fled to Malawi and was not caught.

Working as a volunteer I was given a small allowance each month but I could not survive on the amount of money I received. My accommodation was rent free but food was an expensive commodity. A tin of sardines or a tin of corned beef in Tabora shops cost twenty times the price of the same item in my local supermarket in England. Certain food items were not available in Tanzania at that time. I saw sugar on sale twice in two years; once in a shop in Bukoba, having come across the border from Uganda, and once in Tunduma, brought in from Zambia. At the end of my first year I returned to England for Christmas and New Year. When I stepped on to the bathroom scales at home I discovered a weight loss of two stone, the result of ten months in Tabora.

One day I was looking at household items in a Tabora shop when the Indian owner asked if I would like to change money. In my pocket I did have a few English banknotes and proceeded to take these out. The shopkeeper's hands went up in horror, he waved the notes away and gave me the sign that I should follow him into the back of the shop. The changing of currency, he explained, had to be a covert operation. I did return a number of times to see the same trader, for the same purpose. This allowed me to buy my tins of sardines, corned beef and a few additional items to keep me from any further reduction in weight during my second year in Tabora.

I do enjoy writing letters and even more receiving them. Reading news from friends at home, and from my many friends scattered around the world, is a welcome treat. When staying in my flat in Eastbourne I look forward to the postman's early morning visit but in far-off Tabora, or on one of the three Caribbean islands where I have lived, mail takes on a new importance. It helps me to maintain contact with the people who play an important part in my life. Receiving mail in Tabora was a constant problem. During my two years in Tanzania, approximately twenty-five per cent of my post went missing. Letters and parcels would arrive in Dar es Salaam but something would happen between the capital and the town where I lived. We discovered that a person somewhere on that route enjoyed reading paperbacks. My friend Terry would send a book from England and the package would in due course reach the college. I would write back and say how much I had enjoyed reading *Down and Out in London and Paris*, only to discover in his next letter that Terry had sent a copy of *Murder on the Orient Express*. That postal worker must have enjoyed our book exchange service and must have been sorry when I left Tabora and his reading supply ceased. In one package I was sent four pairs of socks. One member of the post office staff shared the contents so that we ended up with two pairs each. A volunteer friend told me how his mother sent from England slim packets of sliced meat and kippers, rolled in the centre of a magazine. At the time of telling me this good news, all magazines had reached him complete with contents. I decided to try the same system, wrote to my mother and asked if she would send two pillow cases and one tea towel, one item each week, rolled up inside copies of the *Radio Times*. After waiting a month these periodicals started to arrive but the contents were missing, so I never tried that idea again. It happened that I would receive no mail for weeks and then a college friend would come to say, "Mr Roy, is it Christmas or your birthday? You have fifty-eight letters waiting for you in the office."

One day I received a slip of paper from the post office to inform me that a registered letter had arrived and would I collect it? On my arrival at the post office I was taken to a room at the back of the building, where special deliveries were kept, to claim my letter. To my amazement the floor was strewn with express, recorded delivery, and registered letters. I was invited to look for mine, which meant working my way through mail, ankle deep, until the hunt successfully brought me to the discovery of my registered letter. Thinking of the many countries I have lived in, Tanzania has been my worst experience, so far, in the receiving or not receiving of mail.

It was an unusual sight for me to see men walking around in town completely naked. This happened fairly frequently in the centre of Tabora. I noticed that other people took no notice of a man undressed in this way. When I mentioned my surprise to a local friend, who was a magistrate, he told me that there was no law in Tanzania to say that people had to wear clothes. That sounded sensible in a hot climate. After leaving Tanzania I did not meet another naked person parading around until I was staying in Kingston, Jamaica. Walking along the main fashionable shopping streets you would see an occasional naked man, strolling along, with everything swinging and no sign of embarrassment. Once again people around him did not stop to stare as they would in London. When commenting on this to a taxi driver he explained that the naked people we saw, walking or sitting on benches or steps of a building, were drug addicts who did not know what they were doing. I would add here that Kingston, Jamaica was for me the most dangerous capital I have so far visited.

The shortage of food was not the only difficulty which students had to suffer at Tabora Teachers' Training College. Soldiers were members of college staff. An introduction to military training and political party propaganda were part of the college syllabus. The day started with all students assembled on the parade ground. If a student was a few seconds late, he or she had to squat, go down on all fours or lie on the ground, according to instructions, at the edge of the field. From that position students had to hop or crawl to their place in the line up. If a student was slow moving in that ungainly way, or paused for breath, they would be kicked by a heavy army boot. Each morning at break time these latecomers would miss their drink of tea and would have to repeat this process of crawling or hopping along some of the college dirt roads. I would see young female students lying on the ground, trying to pull themselves forward through the mud, their dresses gradually moving further and further up their legs, with soldiers kicking them. Some soldiers seemed delighted if a woman paused for rest. She would be taken away into a small detention room and we never knew what happened to her there. Whatever happened, she would be too frightened to say, afraid that worse would occur later. Students who failed to arrive at morning assembly on time still had one additional punishment. Every Saturday morning, on the parade ground at the back of my bungalow, I would see lines of students marching for three hours in the hot sun with soldiers in attendance. I should perhaps remind readers that these college students were training to be teachers, not soldiers.

Members of the teaching staff also went in fear of their colleagues who were soldiers or those who were members of the political party which ruled Tanzania. One morning during my lecture a student from another department came to say that the new principal wanted my students to leave the class and to go to clean his house. I told the messenger to return to the principal to say that I would not stop my lecture for the students to do his house work. Later that day my head of department came to see me to say that in Tanzania we cannot refuse an order from a person in a higher position. I politely told my department head that I would not have my lectures disrupted in that way. He informed me that in their country people did not have that freedom of choice. If they disobeyed their principal, or a person in a similar position, they would be called to Dar es Salaam and may never return to see their family again. The following day during my lecture another student appeared and informed me that the principal wanted all my students to leave their work and to go to dig in his garden.

Again I refused to release the students. I told my head of department that I was trying to train teachers of the deaf, not gardeners or house cleaners. I never heard another word about this.

It was far easier for me – I could leave Tanzania and work in another country – but unfortunately my fellow lecturers could not escape the system. Most Tanzanians knew what was happening in their country but the single party system denied them any opportunity to express their discontent. There was fear of the Party and Party members. Every school and college had staff and students who were members of the governing party and it was not always known who was a Party member, so no one really knew who was spying on them or when they might be reported to the party and be sent into detention. Not long after my refusal to send students to work in the principal's house and garden, I found my head of department had been given the job, with some students, to dig trenches, eight feet deep, across an area of college ground. This task or punishment lasted a number of weeks. If I needed to see my head on departmental business I had to stand precariously at the edge of the trench where he was working and call down to him items of information concerning our department. Working below ground level he was always afraid that the trench walls would collapse. Later he resigned from college and went into private business.

Students always experienced a shortage of text books. The special education library contained mainly psychology books written around the beginning of this century. One room in college housed a collection of books written in English, but giving the ideology of Kim Il Sung. Fortunately this collection from North Korea appeared to be unopened and unread. There was a general lack of any book in English. No library for students to borrow books for pleasure and to improve, the level of their written and spoken English. The head of the English Department invited me to give a talk to his class. After speaking for five minutes and carefully choosing words I thought the students would know, I paused to find out how many students were really following my presentation. Six students, out of a class of thirty-five, put up their hands to indicate they had understood.

Travel and communications were always a problem in Tanzania. In addition to a doubtful postal service, we did not often find a telephone which worked. Public transport was slow and often broke down. Roads, which were difficult at the best of times, were closed during the wet season. During the dry season, on some roads, you had to dig the vehicle out of the sand. Students living in the south of the country would spend ten days travelling home from college for the three main holidays. This journey would mean a train to the capital, bus along the coast, boat to the south, followed by bus and a final walk to the home village. Students would spend a great deal of time and money travelling home for the three weeks Christmas or Easter break. They stayed a day or two at home with family and friends before making the tiresome, costly, ten day return journey to college. That would be their three week holiday.

One morning the principal announced that Friday would be Graduation Day, when students would receive their diplomas or certificates. This news came as a surprise to me because so far the students had not taken their final examinations. When I mentioned this point to my stressed head of department, he answered by saying that if Graduation Day had been arranged then the students would have to graduate. The great day came and the minister of education arrived, as chief guest, to award a piece of paper to each second year student. When the minister rose to his feet to present his speech, a roll of thunder was heard and down came the rain. The minister spoke for thirty minutes, rain poured down on to the tin roof of the auditorium for thirty minutes. The front row, which contained members of staff, just about caught most of his talk, but the driving rain meant that the whole student population missed every single word. Strange to say when the minister finished talking and eased himself into his seat the rain gradually ceased and out came the sun.

Saturday morning brought a change of routine for students, no lectures and after certain college duties had been completed, they were allowed to go into town. One Saturday I was shopping with my student Assay. After purchasing our needs for that day we went into a small restaurant for refreshments. Assay invited me to go to a basin to wash my hands. I declined and said I had my own water in my pocket. I waited for Assay to rejoin me, then took out of my shirt pocket a sachet containing a wet towelette and preceded to wash my hands. This greatly surprised Assay and on returning to college he told fellow students that Mr Roy carried his own water in his pocket. He was further intrigued in my kitchen when he saw tea bags, sugar, coffee and milk, each in a sachet, and cubes that would crumble to produce soup. One Saturday evening, English friends living in Tabora came to dinner with their six year old daughter. Assay helped me to prepare and serve the meal. The daughter was amazed when Assay sat down at the table to join us for dinner. She turned to her mother to ask what Assay was doing sitting at the table. The youngster had been used to Africans working as servants, but not joining the family at the table. Another of my students was enjoying a meal with me when he announced that I was the first European he had sat with or even spoken to. This was probably true with most of our student population. The majority of Europeans were tourists or diplomats, remote beings from another world.

I mentioned earlier how my bath leaked and flooded the house. A slow trickle of water seeped from one of the supply pipes, flowing out of the bathroom, along the corridor, through the lounge and out of the front door. Every afternoon I would sweep the water from the house and place dry sacks on the floor around the bath. The following day when it came to sweeping time, the flood had once again reached the front door. One afternoon I was sweeping water down the front steps when student friends, Egha and Wilfred, came to visit. They asked if I was having a general spring clean. I explained my daily chore and showed them the source of the problem. They both said that they did not want their tutor to have this daily task and that I should leave it in their hands. The following day and for the rest of the year those two men came daily, without fail, and swept and dried through the house for me. I have unfortunately lost contact with Wilfred, but have continued the friendship with Egha and have visited him a number of times and stayed with his family in Mbeya.

A few minutes walk from our college was a Sisters of Charity Centre. These centres have been set up in many developing countries by Mother Theresa of Calcutta. The sisters cared for more than two hundred residents in Tabora, with ages ranging from new born babies to the very elderly. Frequently an abandoned baby would be found at the gates when they were opened in the morning. Once a week I took the students, training to be teachers of the mentally retarded, to the centre to work with both physically and mentally disabled residents.

Our activities would take the form of hand crafts, reading, conversation, playing with the young children and going for walks. On Saturday afternoons a few of us used to take some of the physically disabled out in their wheelchairs. I remember pushing one young man's chair along the side of a dusty Tabora road when a truck came towards us on the other side. James put both hands over his eyes until the vehicle was almost out of hearing. When I asked James why he had feared the approach of the truck, he said he thought it would hit us. He had not been out of the centre for six years so had not remembered what happened on the roads. I always remember a group of about forty under-fives having tea, but first being disciplined and led in prayer by one of the group just four years of age. Student Egha asked if he could return to the centre in his own time at the weekend.

He explained to us that most of the sisters were from overseas: America, Italy, Ireland, India but all the residents were Tanzanians. He thought that more Tanzanians should help those less fortunate than themselves. Egha went along by himself every weekend to work with the sisters. He would wash bandages, make beds, cut the hair and nails of the old men. I started to teach English to a young quadriplegic man, John Canisio. Eleven years later John and I still exchange letters and greetings cards. He always writes in such a cheerful way.

Mother Theresa went to Tanzania in 1986 to visit the different communities of her Sisters of Charity in the country. She was staying at the Tabora Centre on one of our Tuesday visits. Much to our delight she came around to see us at work. Mother Theresa told me how much she appreciated the help given by the college students and how she welcomed help from members of the local community. She was feeling sad at this time because before arriving in Tabora she had spent a few days with her sisters at their centre in Dadoma. As her aeroplane was leaving Dadoma Airport it somehow swerved and ran into the crowd of well-wishers and tragically killed some of her sisters. Mother Theresa told me that if she had not visited Tanzania then those sisters would still be alive.

My two years at Tabora Teachers' Training College were at an end. When word went around that I would soon be leaving a trail of people came to the house, knocking on my door, to see what I had to sell. Some items I had intended to throw away, such as paper, empty tins and jam jars, were eagerly received. Some household equipment I did sell, mosquito net, oil lamp, crockery and cutlery. On the final day I was eating my last meal, when I heard a lady call "Hodi" at the kitchen door. She explained that she wanted to buy any items I had left. I said I was sorry I had nothing more to sell. She spotted my plate, knife and fork and half eaten meal on the table and insisted she would wait until I had finished and happily take away the unwashed plate and cutlery. At least that saved me washing up.

Chapter Six
Tanzania – On Safari

My first safari from Tabora was to Sekonge, a village sixty miles to the south. Sekonge is known for its hospital, which specialises in the treatment of leprosy. This centre has been supported by the Monravian Church for many years, with nurses and doctors from Denmark and other countries. My visit came about as the result of an individual tutorial which I had one day at college with my student, Assay. We were sitting side by side talking about his latest assignment, when I noticed a problem with one eye. The left pupil had a clear jelly-like growth the size of a small pea. My good friend, Ellen Jensen, a medical sister at Sekonge, used to come to my house on her frequent trips to Tabora. On her next visit to college I mentioned Assay's eye problem and she suggested an examination by an eye specialist at Sekonge. We decided to go for a weekend and take with us four teenage pupils from the local Furaha School for the Blind. Furaha means joy and the children at that school were certainly a happy group.

In Tanzania, when you are about to leave for a journey, people call out "Safari njama", which means "Have a safe trip". We received these farewells from both college students and pupils from Furaha School. First stop on the way to Sekonge was five miles south of Tabora at the David Livingstone Museum. This old Arab house, where David Livingstone lived for six months with H. M. Stanley and a further six months by himself, was a lengthy break in the journey. Our blind school friends enjoyed my verbal descriptions and explanations of all the exhibits, which they were not able to see for themselves.

On arrival at Sekonge, Assay and I were looked after by Ellen, and the four blind pupils were entertained by schoolchildren living at the centre. Sekonge had two schools for pupils whose parents had been cured of leprosy. This was a sad situation. Over the years a large number of people with leprosy had been healed and were no longer a danger to any member of the outside community. They would be discharged from the hospital and return to their home village. In the majority of cases these people would receive a hostile reception and both family and other villagers would chase them away. Village communities did not understand that leprosy could be successfully cured, with ex-patients presenting no risk to other people. They adhered to traditional beliefs that lepers were always outcasts and would remain a threat to the existence of others. With nowhere else to go, these unfortunate people who had been restored to normal health, but rejected by their family and former friends, returned to the shelter of Sekonge. Over the years a large community of cured lepers had grown up in the area. Sekonge was no longer an isolated hospital but now had houses, schools, churches, shops, community centre and a market within this ever growing village.

Our tour of the hospital started with a visit to the men's wards. Ellen said how very pleased the patients would be if we were to shake their hands. Usually visitors kept their distance and made no physical contact. Often they would refuse to enter the patients' rooms. Shaking hands showed that we accepted them and did not reject their touch. She explained that there was no real danger of us catching leprosy. If we did pick up the disease then the modern drugs available today would quickly cure the illness. I had visited a leprosy hospital before, the one at Oji River in eastern Nigeria, when I had gone to see their schools for the blind and physically disabled lepers. Therefore Sekonge hospital presented no fear to me and I was happy to tour the wards meeting all patients, sitting on their beds, shaking hands, or in some cases, shaking what remained of their hands after they had been disfigured by this disabling disease. I noticed that Assay stayed outside each room and watched through a window. In one treatment room patients were having their affected limbs bathed and bandages changed, a daily routine. Some patients had the external parts of their ears and noses eaten away. So many had no fingers or toes, being left with irregular stumps. This situation reminded me of a lady in Japan who complained that she did not have any face powder to decorate her nose. Her protests stopped when her neighbour, an ex-leprosy sufferer, said that she had no nose to powder. The people I met at Sekonge had waited too long before attending hospital for the necessary help. When leprosy is diagnosed during its early stage of growth it can successfully be cured, leaving little permanent disfigurement. Sometimes a person does not realise that he or she has leprosy until they go to pick up something hot, such as a cooking pot from the fire. Then they discover that their hands have been burnt. In these cases leprosy has already taken away their sense of touch. At the end of our meeting with the patients Ellen took us to her own quarters where we gave our hands a good scrub.

Six months later I was home in England and did feel numbness in the fingers of my right hand. I explained to my doctor that I had visited a leprosy centre the previous year. Tests were made but results proved to be negative.

Ellen had a great belief in animal therapy used in a way that would help children who had severe withdrawal symptoms to begin to communicate again. A number of the Sekonge schoolchildren did present problems of a psychological nature, due to their family background. One or both parents had been rejected by society. Some children imitated this and rejected those around them, showing some of the characteristics of autistic children. They displayed a failure to develop social relationships; acting as though they were deaf and resisting learning situations, however interesting these right be. They showed no affection towards another human being, adult or child and they persisted in playing with inappropriate objects. These children had to first learn to want to communicate as most of them seemed more interested in their own small world. Ellen found that a withdrawn child would touch an animal, pick it up or put their arms around it. To hold, cuddle, rock or ride one of the school pets gave pleasure. Children who had stopped talking, started to speak to the cat and dog and began a one-way conversation. It was easier to talk to an animal than to a teacher, parent, brother or sister. The two favourite animals were donkeys because of their docile nature, and rabbits because they were light to hold and soft to hug. However, while standing with arms around the donkey's neck and talking into one of its large, receptive looking ears, children started to join in a conversation with an adult standing close by and even answered some of the questions asked by nurse or teacher.

Our four blind pupils enjoyed the companionship and entertainment provided by their new friends at Sekonge. Gifts had also been prepared by the children, a drum and a long rope made from sisal.

Later, back at their school in Tabora, the drum became a part of the school band and the rope was made into a swing. Assay had his eye examined, treatment was given and the condition cured. During our sixty miles drive over the sandy roads to Tabora we all agreed that it had been a successful weekend safari to Sekonge.

My second safari away from Tabora was really the result of our earlier expedition to Sekonge. Assay asked if I would like to spend a week staying in his village in the south of Tanzania, close to the borders of Zambia and Malawi. I was delighted with the invitation and looked forward to the long annual college holiday. I had to remain at college for a further twelve days to take part in a number of staff duties, so Assay went off on his own to prepare for my visit. We arranged to meet in the town of Mbeya, which was the centre of the Southern Highlands.

As the time approached for my departure I viewed this return rail journey to Dar es Salaam with some trepidation. However, it proved to be fairly uneventful for the majority of passengers. The usual thieves were heard moving about on the roof above us. Some people failed to keep their eyes on their personal possessions the whole time, resulting in lost luggage. One man was killed by falling or being pushed from the train. We arrived in the capital half a day late, so most people thought it was a fairly successful trip.

I remember Ellen telling me about one of her frightening rail safaris between Tabora and Dar es Salaam. She was using a toilet, never a very safe or pleasant experience on those trains, when she overheard two men planning to rob and kill her during the journey. They thought Ellen was a tourist and not conversant with the Swahili language, so they openly planned the robbery. I asked Ellen how she reacted to this situation. She told me that she prayed and arrived safely at her destination. In fact when Ellen heard that I was going to travel to Dar es Salaam by train she made a special visit to college to warn me not to travel first or third class. Second class was the least dangerous she thought, having the company and protection of five other men around me. Assay had travelled the same route the year before. He placed his bag on the overhead rack and spent most of the journey looking in that direction. He must have closed his eyes for a few moments and when he opened them again his bag was gone. This had contained all the clothing he possessed, apart from what he was wearing.

If I had been making my way to the coast during the middle years of the last century, I would have headed towards the town of Bagamoyo. This was the most important coastal town in old Tanganyika, the route taken by the Arabs with their slaves, on their way to the island of Zanzibar. Dar es Salaam was founded by the sultan of Zanzibar as a summer residence. The name Zanzibar has for some time been associated with the growing of cloves. It produces most of the world's cloves and is also known as the Isle of Cloves. To the north of Bagamoyo, close to the border with Kenya, is the port of Tanga. This town gave the name to the whole of the country. Early visitors would arrive in Tanga from places like Mombasa and Zanzibar and point inland and ask the name of the country in that direction. Local people would answer "Tanganyika", meaning "The land beyond Tanga". This name began to be used for the huge area to the south and west of Tanga. When the sultan of Zanzibar was assassinated in a revolution, Julius Nyerere invited the new president of Zanzibar to join Tanganyika to form the United Republic of Tanganyika and Zanzibar. In 1964 the federal state was created with the new name of Tanzania. The president of Zanzibar became vice president of the new republic and a strip of blue, representing the sea surrounding Zanzibar, was added to produce the new flag of Tanzania. In 1973 the government announced that the capital would be moved inland to Dadoma. Nearly twenty-five years later this reluctant move is still in progress.

Tanzania has had a peaceful existence mainly due to the influence and leadership of Julius Nyerere, who became president in 1962. He introduced a single-party state, with elections between rival members of the same party. The Arusha Declaration of 1967 pledged the country to socialist objectives. As the Tanzanian economy deteriorated, Nyerere retired in 1985 handing the leadership over to President Ali Mwinyi, a man from Zanzibar. The new government began to modify its strict policies and gradually introduced a multi-party system. After a period of ten years in office President Mwinyi peacefully handed over power to a new man, an occurrence which is unusual in present day Africa.

Dar es Salaam is not my favourite East African capital. I prefer Kampala and Nairobi with their smarter appearance, great facilities and a general feeling of order, with less congestion on road and pavement, and more safety, certainly now in Kampala. These two cities are also easier for the English-speaking tourist, who perhaps knows little Swahili. The centre of the city of Dar es Salaam has a roundabout where stands the Askari monument in memory of the soldiers of Tanzania who lost their lives during the two World Wars. This area is close to the main hotels, shops and office buildings. It is also the place where most tourists can be seen. Tourists mean money so it is also an area to guard both your pocket and your life. Every time I walked near the Askari monument at least one man would approach me to "Change money?" My reaction was always the same, to keep walking. I heard that those so-called money changers were often police. They began the process of changing money and then showed their police identification. The tourist was then asked for a large on-the-spot fine with the alternative being arrest. Usually the former option was chosen. Walking in the same area with Assay one day we happened to be some yards apart due to looking in different shop windows.

Later Assay informed me that he was approached by a man asking him to help to rob me. Assay explained to the thief that he knew me and that as I had been travelling around the country for many weeks and had very little money, I was not worth robbing. At that same time an Asian tourist was robbed and killed near the Kilimanjaro Hotel. He had been seen in the hotel reception taking a banknote from a bulging wallet to buy a magazine. This man was followed from the hotel into a side street, had a chisel dug into the back of his neck and his wallet taken.

Markets are always interesting places to visit. Dar has a large market with a great variety of goods for sale. I was always intrigued by the use which people in Africa made of items which would be discarded as rubbish in European cities. Disused car tyres were cut up to make sandals. The tyre inner tube cut into strips to make straps to tie around luggage or fasten items on to the backs of bicycles. Tin cans turned into oil lamps, funnels, graters, pastry cutters and the like. Scraps of paper made into envelopes or paper bags. All these items had a ready supply of customers. Most markets would have piles of second-hand clothes. This clothing had come from door to door collections made in Europe by organisations such as Oxfam, Red Cross and Save the Children. Somehow many bales of clothes would find their way into the hands of dealers and the individual items sold at high prices. Students in Tabora would return from the town proudly displaying a second-hand pair of trousers or a dress, bought in the market that day. They would show me a slight fault, perhaps a seam which had become unstitched or buttons missing. The clothing had been given freely in the belief that it would help poor people in the developing world, not to be sold by traders in markets for high prices. I could buy a new pair of trousers in a high street shop in England for less than my students had paid for the second-hand pair in Tabora market. I found the same situation existed in markets in Pakistan. I was taken to a market in Lahore and shown piles of blankets, which had been given freely in Europe to Oxfam, turning up in the market and being sold for a high profit. The same must be happening all over the developing world, traders stealing from the large aid organisations to make themselves rich, instead of these items being given free to the people for whom they were intended.

The railway line from Dar es Salaam to the south was a fairly new line known as the Tanzania–Zambia Railway, or Tazara for short. The railway was built in 1975 with the financial and technical assistance of the People's Republic of China. It was built to help Zambia to export its copper and other products through Tanzania to the coast. Other routes through what was then Rhodesia, Portuguese Mozambique and Angola were closed for political reasons. This railway provided a faster and a far more comfortable journey than the old east–west route. Tazara has its own railway terminal a few miles from the centre of Dar es Salaam.

I travelled as far as Mbeya, where Assay met me at the station. We found a room at the Livingstone Hotel where we stayed for the one night. Mbeya had been an attractive town, with a certain elegance, but that was before independence. Since that time the situation has deteriorated and perhaps the old civic pride has been lost. Now the roads are rutted and potholed. The pavements, which still exist, are in a dangerous condition. Gone are the well kept parks and gardens. Today there is plenty of litter, heaps of rubbish with wildlife, such as goats, rats, crows and the tall, ungainly marabou storks, feeding from the tips. A sad sight for people who knew the area in earlier times.

When Assay reached home the previous week he told his mother that he had invited his college tutor to spend a week with them in their village. His mother welcomed the news until Assay told her that his tutor was a European. She said it was not possible for a white man to live in a mud hut and that she had no food to give him. Assay's home village of Matwabe was situated in the most fertile part of Tanzania. His mother had a market garden covering about one acre. It was no exaggeration to say that the vegetable garden was beautifully kept, a medal-winning example of cultivation. Plants in well tilled lines, like soldiers lined up for inspection, with not a weed to be seen. A great variety of vegetables grew in that moist, cool climate, plus bananas, mango, lemons and avocados, ready to be picked. A plentiful supply of chickens and eggs were also available. With this bountiful harvest at hand Assay listed all the food they had to offer me but still his mother said it was not possible for a white man to live there, not one had ever been seen in the village.

When Assay left home early on the morning of my arrival in Mbeya, his mother still did not believe that I would return with Assay the following day. I asked Assay if there was a village bus which would take us home. He assured me that the village did possess a bus. When I asked if we would be using the bus he said, "No!" When I asked why he said because it had no wheels. People did not like to admit that they did not have, or could not do, something. At the college when I asked my head of department if the college had a shop where I could purchase a few things, he said yes, they had a shop. I asked if he would take me to see it but he answered by saying that it was not open at that time of day. I next asked the opening time and was told 5 p.m. When I inquired about the closing time I was again told 5 p.m. So from that information I gathered that there was no shop at college but my department head did not like to admit the fact.

I walked with Assay into his village and we made for a house where I saw a lady standing at the front door. I asked if it was correct procedure to shake hands with his mother and was told yes, that was allowed. When I approached his mother with my hand held out, she disappeared inside the hut and closed the door. Assay explained that she could not shake hands and welcome a visitor outside because a visitor brought good luck but if hands were shaken outside, then the good luck would fly away. A hand shaken inside the hut would mean the good luck would remain. When we entered we found his mother on her knees waiting to greet us. The custom with many tribes in East Africa is for the woman to welcome a man in a kneeling position, even a mother greeting her son. Living in the same house were Assay's adult sister, Elizabeth and one of his young nephews, Kevin.

During my stay with Assay, we two were given the main hut to live in while his mother, Elizabeth and Kevin had their meals and slept in the kitchen.

Word soon went around that a European man was living in the Shibanda hut, news which brought many people to look to see if it was true. Villagers found this a very strange situation, especially the old people. They would look through the open wooden shutters, clap their hands and rock with laughter. Young men entered the hut to look at some of my modern gadgets: a camera with a zoom lens; a digital short wave radio; noisy battery-operated razor; an exciting computer game which became well used, and a torch which could also operate a flashing red light. The battery operated razor proved to be the most popular, which brought a line of men each morning waiting for me to give them a shave.

Before leaving Mbeya I had asked Assay to choose a gift which he thought his mother would like to receive. Without hesitation he suggested a kanga. This is the garment worn by the majority of ladies in Tanzania and some neighbouring countries. Opened to its full length it would be about the size and shape of a single bed sheet but there the similarity ends. The kanga is light in weight, usually made from cotton and highly decorative in appearance. Some show a kaleidoscope of colours, others depict national emblems, slogans or the portrait of their president. Being worn around the waist or higher if a baby is being carried on the back, it was not uncommon to see the face of Kenneth Kaunda, Hastings Banda or Julius Nyerers, bouncing up and down on a rotund lady's back, bottom or stomach, as though their raised hand was really waving a greeting to us. Entering a shop selling kangas was like walking into an Aladdin's cave of colours with hundreds of cloths draped from ceiling and walls. The choice of kanga was left to me so I purchased one with colours more suited to an older lady, a mixture of yellow and browns, with a patriotic slogan around the edge.

An English friend in Tabora bought herself a kanga but thought the article looked too attractive to be worn so she placed it on her sitting room wall as a decoration. One afternoon two women friends from school came to visit. When they entered the sitting room they could not stop themselves from laughing at the kanga on the wall. My friend asked why it seemed such a funny thing to do. The visitors asked if she would in England hang a pair of trousers on the wall as a decoration because the kanga was just something to wear.

Assay's mother was of course delighted with her gift and put it carefully away in her cupboard, but it appeared again to be proudly shown to each of the many visitors we received that week.

Sitting under the avocado tree, we had a fine view across a valley to the distant range of Livingstone Mountains. It was a delight to see so much lush foliage all around us after living in dry Tabora. One morning sitting under the tree I saw Assay's mother arrive at the front of the hut carrying a heavy basket containing a large amount of cow dung. I am not sure now if I identified it first by sight or smell. The basket was emptied at the front door and more baskets brought. I watched the pile grow and wondered what would happen next. Tins of water were poured on to the dung and his mother mixed the solid and liquid together with her hands until it became a paste-like substance. I turned to Assay to ask what his mother was doing. He explained that she wanted to make my sleeping area smart so she would spread this mixture over the mud floor around the bed where I slept. At first I did not believe this but it soon happened. Elizabeth followed her mother and with their bare feet the surface of wet dung was pressed into shape. The final touch was made by Elizabeth when she produced a pattern on the drying excrement with a pronged stick. Now I had a carpet of decorated dung at either side of my bed. I waited a number of hours, for the surface to dry, the air to waft away the last of the smells and for the flies to satisfy themselves before entering the room. After this I started to notice around the village that cow dung was regularly used to strengthen walls of houses, both interior and exterior and patterns would decorate the surfaces.

When two people of different ages met the usual greeting was for the younger one to say to the older "Shkamoo", a Muslin greeting which really means "I kiss your feet". The answer to this is "Marhaba", "You may kiss my feet". Most younger people meeting me, or children just in passing, would say "Shkamoo", and I would give the appropriate answer. One difference was the younger children below the age of five years. When they saw me fear would be shown and away they would run. If walking with an adult the youngster would keep close, hold on to the mother or hide on the other side of the parent. Some mothers would hold or try to push their child in jest towards me and then the little one would scream and shake in genuine fear. When I first experienced this in Tabora I asked my students why were children afraid of white people. They explained that the mother was at fault. She would threaten her child that if he or she misbehaved then a white man would come with a large bag to put them in and carry them away. Therefore, when I was seen, young children must have wondered what they had done wrong and that I would disappear with them. I laughed at this answer because it reminded me of the time when I was about four years of age my mother had said the same, things to me, only the colour was different. She threatened me that if I misbehaved a black man would come with a big sack to put me in to take me away.

Every day I would play a little with Assay's nephew Kevin. One morning I chased him and he ran away. A few minutes later he was back at the hut so in fun I chased him again. This time he froze and screamed. Assay had to come to calm him down and to reassure Kevin that I meant him no harm. His reaction surprised me because after all those days together I thought he had accepted me and enjoyed our games.

Most people in the rural areas on Tanzania live at a subsistence level, they grow their own food, make their own shelter, sell a little home grown produce and use the proceeds to purchase extra items such as metal tools and clothing. The main cash crops are cotton, tea and coffee. Ujamaa was one of Julius Nyerere's dreams. This was when all people from the isolated villages would collect together in much larger groupings. These new Ujamaa villages would provide a school, clinic and communal water supply. Communities were driven at gun point into newly formed villages and their old family homes burnt down and lands lost There was much resistance around the country to this policy. The people in Matwabe village and many others in that border territory refused to follow the plan and escaped without any further harassment. Matwabe had a communal water supply but Assay would never show this to me. Elizabeth or her mother collected their water but I never followed. If it was anything like some of the swamps we used later in Uganda to collect our drinking water then I am not surprised at his reluctance.

Assay and I would eat our meals together inside the hut while the women and Kevin ate in the kitchen. The women would prepare, cook and serve the food and then depart: that was the custom. Some evenings Assay's friends would join us for a meal followed by cards.

The main topics of conversation on those occasions were politics, religion, sport and girlfriends, perhaps the same all over the world when men come together. A few hours of card playing could be a strain on the eyes because the only light available for six men sitting around the table with their hands full of cards came from the small flame of one home made oil lamp. When Assay's mother and Elizabeth had finished their kitchen chores and brought sufficient water to begin the next day, they were then free to enter the hut and sit on the floor together in one corner. The table lamp gave out so little light that it was not possible to see far beyond the edge of the table. The rest of the room remained in total darkness. The only way we knew the women were there was by the occasional sound of one of their voices. In the villages people would go to bed early when all household duties had been completed for the day. We got up when the sun rose, or I should say I got up when I was told that hot water was ready for my morning bath.

Most village days followed the same pattern: collecting water and firewood, preparing meals, feeding chickens, working in the shamba, chatting with friends. Sometimes there was a little excitement. One morning I heard Elizabeth give a scream and saw Assay run with sheets of newspaper. He proceeded to set these on fire and drop the burning paper on to the ground. The cause of the disturbance, was an army of soldier ants making their way, in a wide column, towards the house. Brother and sister were trying to use fire to change their direction, a very difficult thing to do once these creatures had determined the direction they wanted to go. The burning newspaper failed to prevent the march to the house but oil from the lamp, set on fire, made the ants change their route.

Later that day I asked Assay if he knew how to make fire the traditional way by rubbing two sticks together. He said this was an easy task. He collected two sticks, one of soft wood, one of hard, some dry grass and small dry twigs. His hands moved at a rapid pace twisting the point of the hard stick into the soft wood. Within a very short time smoke started to rise from the soft stick, helped along by our gentle blows of air. Dry grass was added which smoked for a few seconds before it burst into small flames. Finally twigs were added to the grass and we had a fire, a process which took about four minutes from start to finish. I tried to follow Assay's demonstration to make my own fire but my hand action was not fast enough to produce even the tiniest puff of smoke. If I was lost in the forest by myself I would have to survive on uncooked food and unboiled water.

My week in Matwabe came to an end. I asked Assay if he thought his sister Elizabeth would like to return to Tabora with me to look after my college house. He asked and she agreed. After many "Safari njamas" from family and friends the two of us travelled together, this time by bus to Mbeya and continued by a second bus to Dar es Salaam. This was Elizabeth's first visit to the capital where we had to spend some days in a hotel before I managed to buy the necessary railway tickets to Tabora. Spending all her life in a small village, which had neither electricity nor running water, Elizabeth did not know how to work a light switch or turn on a tap. These two processes were easy to learn but often she did not remember to turn off the switch or bathroom taps. Early one morning I got out of bed to go to the hotel bathroom, put my feet on to the floor to find that a flood of water covered my ankles. As I walked my feet sent waves of water across the bedroom floor. A pair of sandals were floating on top of the water. Elizabeth had gone to the bathroom during the night, washed her hands but left the water tap turned on. We flooded five other hotel bedrooms.

This situation reminded me of a visit I made to Port Harcourt in the Rivers State of Nigeria. I was visiting my friend Jean, who taught at a school in the town. One Saturday afternoon Jean and I visited a cinema with the son and daughter of two of her Nigerian friends who were studying in England. The cinema was situated in a fine five-star hotel, used by many of the overseas oil workers in that area. During the interval Jean took the girl along to the toilets and I took the twelve year old boy. When we entered what seemed to him a marble palace, he could not believe that we should urinate in such beautiful surroundings. In his village he would carry out the same function by using a hole in the ground or by going behind a bush. I had to demonstrate by urinating first to let him see how we used the facility before he diffidently followed my example.

During our stay in Dar es Salaam, Elizabeth enjoyed going with me to cinemas, restaurants and walking along the sea front. One evening, after a restaurant dinner, we were about to enter the hotel when a new night porter stopped us at the front door and asked me for some money. At first I could not understand why, then I quickly realised that he thought I was taking a prostitute back to the hotel to spend a night. I soon explained that we both had rooms booked at the hotel.

In that area of the capital many prostitutes could be found on the streets. I also saw one male prostitute dressed in such a way that he advertised his interest in offering his services to other men. This open display was unusual in East African towns.

For some years I had been wanting to visit Gombe Stream. This is a centre for the study of chimpanzees in the wild, established more than twenty-five years ago by Jane Goodall. I had read her book, *In The Shadow Of Man*, seen her television programmes, heard Tabora friends speak about their visit to see the chimpanzees and had seen the video they had produced. I had even collected the stamp which featured one of the most popular Gombe chimps. Now I wanted to make my own visit.

Once again I travelled with Assay, but it was a year after we made our first visit to Matwabe. Assay was by then a teacher at the Bukoba School for the Deaf and joined me for another safari during the long school, college holiday period. After spending a few days together at my college house, we took the train west from Tabora to Kigoma on the shores of Lake Tanganyika. The first part of our journey took us through a dry, fairly barren area which had changed in appearance over the previous twenty years. My college friend, Brother John, remembered this district when it was mainly covered by thick forest. The two main factors which led to this present state of deforestation were goats destroying the young trees and men chopping down the older trees, mainly for firewood. The work of men and goats had brought about a dry, dusty landscape. Throughout most of the regions of Dadoma and Tabora there is a high incidence of blindness. I feel sure that some of the diseases which cause blindness are windborne. Dust-laden winds would blow through Tabora almost daily. I always wore sunglasses when going out of the house, for both cutting down on the glare of the fierce sun and for keeping some of the dust and germs out of my eyes. The more trees cut down the less rain received so both these regions had drought problems. When the prayed-for rain fell at college students would rush out with their buckets, pans or any container available to catch the precious drops. In Tabora I had my first night time rain shower. When it was dark and the rain was falling I would step almost naked from the house, wearing just my sandals and carrying a bar of soap. An enjoyable shower of cool rain would follow which meant that some of the rainwater collected earlier could be saved for other uses. I did have running water on tap in the house but when the local system broke down our own supply was a valuable asset.

Soon after leaving Tabora by train the traveller became aware of trees containing large logs hanging from ropes suspended twenty feet or more from the ground. At first I thought it might be the result of children playing a game but after seeing a second and a third tree with a log hanging in the same way, I started to think it might be for another purpose. Assay explained that was the local way of collecting honey. If you mention the name Tabora to a beekeeper who knows the main honey harvesting areas of the world, he will start talking about the different way honey is collected in that region.

During the years when Tanganyika was a German colony it was realised that this part of the country was an important source of beeswax and honey. In the old days local people used to kill all the bees then extract the honey. A new way was recommended, saving the bee colonies when the honey was taken. Today the hives are suspended using a forked stick attached by two wires. Traditional log hives are made by hollowing out a section of tree trunk with a home made tool. Some owners burnt their own brand name or symbol on to the outside so as to identify their hive. Both ends of the log are almost closed but a hole, large enough for the worker bees but not the queen bee to pass through, is left. Evenings are the time for collecting honey when the bees are quieter. Bees seem to store their honey at the top end of the log, so this end was opened first. Large wads of smouldering grass were used to smoke the bees while the honey was removed. The log was then once again hauled back to its original position.

In 1982 FAO (Food and Agriculture Organisation) estimated that Tanzania was the second largest exporter of honey and beeswax in Africa. With the vegetation in Central Tanzania becoming more sparse I should think the output of honey would be on the decline. I have always enjoyed honey for breakfast every day and a spoonful in each cup of herbal tea. When I offered honey to Assay's sister, Elizabeth, when she stayed with me in the college house, she refused to eat it. I discovered the reason for this rejection was that an uncle had died from a bee sting inside his mouth when he was extracting honey from one of his home-made log hives.

When we reached the town of Kigoma we had come to the end of the line. That night we stayed in the Kigoma Railway Hotel in a room booked by one of my students. All the railway hotels I stayed in during safaris around Tanzania proved to be satisfactory. Tabora Railway Hotel was built last century as the main hunting lodge in East Africa for members of the German Royal Family. Kigoma is the main Tanzanian town on the shores of Lake Tanganyika, the second deepest freshwater lake in the world. A few years later when travelling in Siberia I sailed across Lake Baikal, the world's deepest freshwater lake. If I had visited Lake Baikal in winter I could have driven across by bus or car, due to the water freezing to such a great depth. During the war years railway lines crossed the lake in winter, a very different scene from hot, humid Lake Tanganyika and its surroundings. Across the lake we could see the shores of Zaire. To the north lay Burundi and Zambia to the south. Close to Kigoma is the village of Ujiji, made famous last century by the meeting of two British-born gentlemen, Livingstone and Stanley.

On our return from Gombe Stream we encountered another piece of history when we sailed on a boat going to Zambia. This riverboat was brought to German Tanganyika in pieces at the beginning of this century. It was transported from the coast to Kigoma, where it was assembled on the lake. For a period of ten years, until the outbreak of the First World War, this boat sailed up and down the vast lake with its first-, second- and third-class passengers. During the war years the British managed to bomb the vessel, which sank to the bottom of the lake. When hostilities were over and Tanganyika became a British territory, the new authorities salvaged the boat, cleaned and repaired it until we had the fine old boat we see today following its original route once again. Assay and I shared a first-class deck cabin for two on our overnight journey south. When I looked around the historic cabin I admired the German workmanship of those early years, with a mixture of wood with its rich grain still looking fresh and the bright shine of the brass fittings. It was a delight not to see one piece of chipboard, Formica, plastic or plywood.

To reach Gombe we had to discover which one of many small motor-powered boats headed north for this journey, which under normal conditions, lasted about two hours. Many boats were to be found along the shore leading from Kigoma but it was a puzzle to know which one to take to the chimpanzee sanctuary. One boat owner would say in Swahili words which meant "Do not go with that man, he will rob you". Another captain would point to the neighbouring boat and say, "That boat is old, it will sink." One man would try to take hold of my hand and pull me in one direction while another boat owner began to collect our luggage to carry off to place in his vessel. I suggested to Assay that we found out which boats were going to Gombe Stream, guess which would be the first to leave, because there were other passengers going in the same direction, and then we could sit ourselves and our luggage in that boat and hope for the best. This idea partly worked but when a number of fellow passengers, including ourselves, had been sitting in one boat for half an hour, the owner decided he would not leave that day so we all had to disembark to another boat which seemed to be showing signs of imminent departure. Once again we were frustrated, this owner lost interest in a journey that day and recommended his brother's boat. Our move was less optimistic but turned out to be third time lucky. Within another hour we started to pull away from Kigoma with a stuttering engine. At last we were on our way. Two and a half hours later fellow passengers told us that around the next bend in the coast line we would see Gombe Stream. We had to shout to the captain our wish to stop. Boats did not make regular visits to Gombe, but would call if a passenger wanted the Sanctuary. We were warned to be ready at eight o'clock on the morning of our departure and to be on the lookout for a boat travelling south. We should then wave our arms and hope someone on board would see us so that we could be collected and returned to Kigoma.

We stood on Gombe beach with our numerous pieces of luggage. The reason we had so many bags was the need to take our own food and bedding to the Sanctuary. Accommodation and amenities provided consisted of kitchen, with cooking utensils and a supply of dry firewood, bedrooms with beds and mattresses. We arrived with essential mosquito nets, bedlinen and all food required during a stay of four days. There were no shops or markets in the area for purchasing supplies, although it was possible to buy fresh fish from the men when they were bringing their daily catch on to the beach. The cost of renting a room for the night was most reasonable, just a few shillings for each evening of our stay at the centre. Assay took over the job of fire lighter and cook. My work contribution was the preparation of some food and washing up. Dishes and pots and pans we washed in the fresh, clear water of the stream which gave Gombe National Park part of its name.

The rest house buildings were well protected from the marauding baboons which frequented this area, mainly in large family groups dominated by a large male. We were the ones inside large cages looking out on the animals, which were completely free. Assay used to laugh at this almost unique situation of the baboons coming to the windows to look at him taking part in his kitchen duties. A young male would hold its hand to the wire hoping to receive a piece of fruit or vegetable. The whole time its eyes would be looking to left and right in case a larger male appeared, as usually happened. A minor skirmish would take place with the younger male frequently receiving a bite. Every morning a family of about twenty baboons would make its way through the trees, across the roof of our hut, with the thud of many feet, on their way to drink at the stream. We were told not to encourage the baboons to the hut by giving titbits to eat. It had been known for a large male to carry away a young human child, which would be eaten.

Every morning a guide came to take us to the main observation areas just a few minutes walk from the rest houses, to wait and watch for the arrival of the chimpanzees. The main attraction for the chimps were the individual bananas placed in a container which also doubled as a weighing machine. Members of staff were in attendance to record all that happened to the chimpanzees while they were in that viewing area. Each animal could be recognised by staff and was known by name. Therefore a note could be written in the book to say that Peter weighed so many pounds that morning. A tape recorder would register the grunts, calls or any other noise made, such as the attack we witnessed one morning when a young male showed a display of anger by hitting a metal drum. This type of behaviour, which was perhaps a little different from say Bobo's daily routine, would be faithfully recorded. Over the years a valuable biography was compiled of each member of the large family groups which inhabited the Gombe Reserve.

When park staff decided it was the end of the feeding session for that morning we were taken by our guide to follow the tracks taken by the chimpanzees and were able to see them feeding, at play or sleeping in branches of their favourite trees. Sometimes we were part of a foot patrol, a chimp taking the lead followed by a park warden,

Assay and finally myself trying to keep up with those ahead of me. Gombe Stream did not receive a large number of visitors at that time which meant that we had the park to ourselves, not forgetting, of course, the staff and animals.

Jane Goodall's wide-ranging and detailed research into the life and behaviour of chimpanzees at Gombe Stream is now world-famous. Both Jane and Dian Fossey of Rwanda fame, where she studied the mountain gorilla, started their work in Africa in a similar way. They were helped by the famous African anthropologist Louis Leakey, who responded positively to their enthusiasm for working with primates in Africa. In her book *In The Shadow Of Man* Jane Goodall told us of her unexpected discovery that chimpanzees used tools. She observed chimps taking sticks to termite nests, where they would poke the stick into termite holes to skewer the termites and then stick the insects into their mouths. Before this startling discovery it was thought that man was the only animal to use tools to assist him with his every day tasks. A later discovery, which was described in another of Jane Goodall's books, *The Chimpanzees Of Gombe – Patterns of Behaviour*, spoke about her horror when she observed a planned, deliberate and prolonged attack by one group of chimpanzees upon another group which had broken away some years before. She was certain that the Gombe group had set out to destroy others of their own kind, something which was not known in the animal kingdom, apart from man, who was supposed to be of a higher intelligence. She saw how a group of males went to search for and found animals of a neighbouring group. This raid was planned and systematically carried out. A member of the opposite group was held, jumped on, and bitten until it died. This killing was of both males and females, with some of the young ones being eaten. This warfare fundamentally altered her perception of chimpanzee society from the ordered, peace loving group she thought she knew. This also brought them, in her eyes, closer to *Homo sapiens*. One of Jane Goodall's areas of study now is to see how the early experiences of baby chimps affect them as they grow into adulthood. If a baby does not receive love and affection from its mother, does this coldness stay with the chimp and result in bad mothering later on?

Early on the morning of our fourth day at Gombe Stream Assay was out on the beach, well before the expected eight o'clock arrival time, to watch for a boat coming from Brundi in the north on its way to Kigoma. Assay forgot he was in Tanzania, where African time is the order of the day. While he was anxiously patrolling the shoreline, I sat on a flat rock under a tree and read a book. I did not see the need for two of us to be worried by the lateness of the boat and the fact we had another boat to catch to sail to Zambia later in the day. At ten o'clock, when Assay was wishing that we had departed the day before, our friendly park guide came to join us and said that the boat would arrive soon. As the vessel came into view we were told to wave in its direction to catch the attention of passengers or crew.

On our way to Kigoma the engine started to splutter and came to a halt. It took the captain some time to discover the fault and to begin his repair. I tried to reassure Assay, by showing him my watch, that we still had plenty of time before the departure of our next transport. When we had been chugging along for about another fifteen minutes, and we experienced yet another engine failure, I also began to doubt our chances of arriving at our destination on time. Now it became more difficult to restore and maintain Assay's confidence in Tanzanian expertise in mechanical repairs. Fortunately our second interruption was just a slight pause and no more delays were encountered until we came to the last bay and promontory before Kigoma. The boat slowed down and a man with his trousers rolled up above his knees leapt into the water with a bag on his head and waded ashore. I wondered why he had not continued his journey with us until I saw customs officials checking all bags when we left the boat at Kigoma. We had sufficient time for a meal at the Railway Hotel before boarding the historical old ship for our journey to Zambia, so Assay was happy.

During my two years in Tanzania I had one working safari. This was when I took the students to Dar es Salaam for their six week block teaching practice. With all railway journeys, as soon as I knew my safari dates, without any delay I would go to see the station master to persuade him to let me have the necessary papers which would allow me to purchase the required tickets for that dreaded train journey on the east–west line. On the morning of our departure I had eleven second-class tickets safely placed in my pocket. We carried sufficient food to last the group for at least two days of travel. Each student had been given a part of their personal spending allowance. A separate bag had been packed with teaching materials. I had warned three students that I did not want alcohol to spoil their chances of a successful completion of this practical part of their training. So as we waited for the train to arrive from Mwanza, a large town on the shores of Lake Victoria, I felt fairly confident that we were heading for what should prove to be a satisfactory teaching practice at Burguruni School for the Deaf.

Our train gradually rolled into Tabora station with third-class carriages situated at the rear. Seats in third class were not booked so the first passengers into the compartment had a choice of seat. Those who arrived later could choose between standing or sitting on the floor. As a result of this a mass of excited people would jump on to the steps of the moving train, resulting in a sprawl of arms and legs flying in all directions and luggage getting tangled up in this melee of eager passengers hoping for a seat. Other people would climb through windows, so that each window space would present a vast congestion of heads, arms, bottoms, legs and feet at different angles and in various stages of twisting and somersaulting into the train. When you add to this women with their kangas flowing, trying to hold on to babies and small children, live chickens, restrained by a single piece of string, chaos reigned for some time. Fortunately I never saw a goat taken on to a train as I have seen travelling with their owners in some forms of road transport.

One trick I have seen men use to try to gain a seat in a third-class carriage is to seek the aid of non-travelling friends. Your friends enter different compartments, either through windows or doors and engage in the process of fighting for a seat. If one is successful he shouts out for you to enter that carriage. When you find him you exchange seats and wish him a grateful thanks and goodbye. The more friends available, the more chance you have of gaining a seat for the journey.

We had no need to hurry because our eleven seats were safely booked, or so we thought. I should have known from previous experience that a train ride to the capital would not be that easy. When we found the carriage where we had our booking we could see from the platform that every seat had been occupied by soldiers, not one to spare. In frustration I hurried off to find the busy stationmaster who was occupied trying to solve some of the many travel problems which arose on a day when a train departed. He was aware of our difficulty and when he saw me, came to explain that soldiers were on their way from Mwanza to Dar es Salaam to take part in military manoeuvres and all second-class seats throughout the train had been requisitioned by the army. In Tanzania, as in most African countries, you do not argue with the military, you accept the problems they impose. The only thing I could do to further my argument was to say that we would not travel that day and demanded the return of our money. I knew that the ticket money would never be reimbursed but hoped we might gain something by my threats. My ploy worked and the stationmaster said we could have the one compartment which was usually reserved for staff. This contained seating for eight adults, at a squeeze, but I quickly accepted before that was taken by other distressed travellers, who found themselves in the same unhappy state. I explained the facts to my students, who were far from happy with the situation because soldiers were not the most popular people in the country. My charges entered the carriage where we had our original booking and started to make their way between the seats of soldiers to where we had our new accommodation.

The next thing I became aware of was student Constantine having a heated argument with three soldiers who were trying to push him towards the carriage exit. Apparently he had said something abusive to upset the men and now they were determined to throw him off the train. I tried to force myself between Constantine and the soldiers with calls to leave him alone because he was travelling with me. This squabbling procession reached the door where the three soldiers were down on the platform trying to pull a reluctant student off, with myself still inside the train, balanced on the top step with Constantine, trying to pull him back inside again. The soldiers won and we both had to jump off on to the platform. Now that we were by ourselves I told Constantine to be quiet and to say nothing. I would take his hand and together we would walk through the carriage in silence and hope we would not be stopped. I explained to him how important it was for all of us to arrive in Dar es Salaam to take part in the coming teaching practice. Fortunately this action worked and we gained our seats.

Students found two pieces of wood which were placed between the seats so that all eleven passengers in that compartment at least could sit down but I doubted if there would be much sleep that night. As the train chugged out of the station and "Safari njamas" were shouted to the students by college friends, I sat back in my seat, closed my eyes for a few moments and thought back twenty years. I could not remember my tutor in Manchester suffering any of those difficulties when she took her students off to teaching practice in schools for the deaf in Birmingham.

We made good time to Dadoma and continued on our way to Morogoro, the last large town before reaching Dar. Morogoro had an important sisal industry. This is the fibre used in the making of rope, twine and similar products. Tanzania was the world's leading sisal producer but the trade has declined with the introduction of man-made fibres. Fields of sisal can still be seen around Morogoro but the crop is no longer an important earner of foreign currency.

Between Morogoro and Dar the train made two abrupt stops because a man had fallen off the train each time and had been killed. This seemed to be a common occurrence on these railway journeys. At a third halt I heard a number of gunshots coming from the carriage next to us. I went to investigate and found soldiers shooting out of windows at some rocks a few feet away from the side of the train. Taking a closer look I discovered the reason for the excitement. Snakes had chosen those rocks to bask in the sun and were the objects of the soldiers shooting. As the train pulled away more snakes came into view and the soldiers continued their target practice. This reminded me of the American Western films when cowboys or soldiers used to shoot out of train windows at attacking Indians. When I watched those films I was always on the side of the Indians. During that journey to Dar es Salaam I was not sure if I was on the side of the snakes or the soldiers, both could prove to be fatal. When our journey ended we were just three hours late, not a record but a fairly good arrival time. Two passengers had died on the way, snakes had been shot, we had lost all our booked seats to the soldiers and those were just the events I knew about. I am sure if other passengers had been asked to contribute they could have added to this list of hazards of travel.

One week prior to our departure for teaching practice the head of our section at college went to Dar es Salaam to arrange accommodation for students and staff. We did not expect to be housed in the Kilimanjaro Hotel, the top hotel in the capital at that time, but we expected a basic standard of comfort and hygiene. When we saw the hut provided and its lack of facilities we were dismayed. The wooden building consisted of one room, which contained twenty-four beds and two buckets. Our number had grown to twenty-four because we were joined by students from other college departments, also taking their teaching practice at that time. One of our buckets was expected to cater for all the washing and bathing needs of twenty-four men and the second was our toilet. To add to our discomfort each wall had many windows without curtains. The hut was situated between two busy roads with a connecting path running along one side of the building. This presented a free exhibition for passers-by. I explained to the section head that there was not a table or chair for students to use for lesson preparation, and no privacy because there were no curtains. I asked how was it possible for so many men to wash in one bucket and to have just one bucket for a toilet. I explained how sickness would develop and spread. The answer I received was that we were living in Tanzania and not England.

The main thing which concerned the students was that their tutor would suffer in those appalling conditions. I explained that I would remain with them and would try to see how we could improve the situation. The following day students came to me to say they had found a free staff room for me to use at Buguruni School and they would move my luggage so that I could begin my stay there that day. I did leave the hut for the private room at school but also managed to improve the students' accommodation.

I arranged for them to have a morning wash and evening shower at the nearby residential school for the blind and also to use their toilets, doubled the number of buckets to four which were used for washing clothes, covered windows to a certain height with newspaper for necessary privacy, borrowed tables and chairs for evening study work, and arranged for students to prepare lessons in classrooms during and after school hours. During the first week one student became ill with amoebic dysentery, which needed hospital treatment. If the level of hygiene which we encountered on our arrival had lasted throughout the six weeks of teaching practice then most of the students would have become seriously ill.

Education is free at all levels in Tanzania, although it is not compulsory. Most of the schools are run by the government but some are owned by missions. Because of a shortage of school buildings and teachers only about half of Tanzanian children enter primary schools. A small percentage of teenagers attend secondary schools. Figures issued in 1996 by Save the Children, show that Tanzania spent six times more money annually on defence than on health. If the country at least halved its defence budget and used that money on health and education then we would see a rise in the number of healthy children attending primary and secondary schools. If we look at one neighbouring country Malawi, we see that they spend $2.50 per head annually on defence and a larger amount, $3.80 per head, on health.

Children in Tanzania follow a primary programme lasting seven years. Pupils at a school for the deaf were allowed to extend their primary school years by three to give them ten years of education.

If a child entered school at five years of age, he or she would then receive full time, usually residential, education until the age of fifteen. However, a child rarely went to school at that early age; the usual age of admission was around the eighth birthday. Some students joined school for the first time as old as ten, twelve or in some cases fourteen years. The head boy when I was staying at Buguruni School was twenty-four years old. Samuel had started school at fourteen and automatically stayed until he had completed his ten years.

I was impressed by the way in which deaf children at Buguruni willingly took part and took pride in their out-of-school duties. These activities included: making their beds; cleaning their accommodation; washing their own clothes; assisting in the dining room; and, with some of the older boys, looking after about five hundred chickens. The standard of behaviour in the classrooms and in general around the school was higher than I had seen in schools in Europe and North America. The students also displayed a greater sense of maturity at all age levels. It was a pleasure to see how the older pupils helped the younger ones in these activities. Samuel would bring a bucket of water to my room each morning to throw over the concrete floor and then sweep out the water. Twice a day he brought my meal to the room, lunches I had in the school dining room with pupils and staff.

In addition to classroom teaching I encouraged my teachers in training to take their class out for day trips and I would accompany them to lend an extra pair of hands. One morning I was with one student and eight pupils on a fairly crowded bus going into the centre of Dar. My head spent most of the time swivelling around to keep all eight pupils in sight. I remember asking the student how he would always like to have eight children to look after. He informed me that he had nine children of his own at home. One of our outings was to the national museum. This was a large, old colonial building with many rooms but few exhibits, not really worth a visit, unlike the national museums in Kampala and Nairobi.

Every weekend we would try to have a break from school and often made our way to a restaurant followed by the cinema. Students were all of the same opinion that European women were immoral because they walked around towns in nothing but their underwear. This idea came about from watching films, mainly from America, which showed women at seaside resorts dressed in bikinis. I tried to explain the use of this beachwear but it did not change their ideas about promiscuous European women.

Dar es Salaam had some historical sites which included the boma, an old fort facing the harbour. This would have made an interesting tourist attraction but during the days of our teaching practice it was closed to the public, being in a state of disrepair. Soon after restoration work started, but when I made a visit ten years later work had not been completed.

Dar's main market covered an extensive area. One Saturday morning when shopping in the market with the students, we noticed a boy of about seven years of age being chased and caught by another boy of about twelve. A beating took place and the younger boy was being severely injured. I asked the students if we could stop this fight and possible killing but they said no. They explained that it was the law of the streets, the younger boy had been seen stealing and this was his punishment. If we intervened we would be in danger of being attacked ourselves by the crowd of bystanders which had gathered around us.

My friend Ellen visited Dar es Salaam during teaching practice so I invited her along to school to give a talk about the leprosy centre at Sekonge, to college students plus members of school staff. Pictures were shown and Ellen described the different stages of leprosy and the treatment patients received. To my amazement and embarrassment students and teachers started to smile and laugh. The more severe the disfiguration shown on the screen the more the audience laughed. I could not understand how they could react in that way. Later when I talked with Ellen and tried to apologise for the way the students responded, Ellen said she understood their reaction. The laughter was, she said, a way of hiding their true feelings over the horrors and suffering shown. It was a way of masking their emotions.

I was invited to attend a meeting of the 'Group of Four'. This was an organisation representing four different groups of disabled people: deaf, blind, physically disabled and the albino. The albino being classed as a disabled person was something I did not understand before going to Africa. If you are an albino with white skin, blond hair, pink eyes and live in a country in Western Europe, then you blend fairly easily with other fair-skinned people in that country. However, being an albino in Africa is a very different situation. They have the same albino colouring but African facial features and hair texture. The albino is generally not accepted by the African because of his or her pale skin and in most cases not accepted by the European community living in Africa because he or she is African. In some African countries the albino is spoken of as the 'child of the devil'. The belief is that the baby was born with the same features and colouring as the parents but during the night the devil came and stole away the newborn child and placed one of his own children, the albino, in its place. One of my students told me that a cousin of his was an albino. He had tried to make a living by selling his home-grown fruit and vegetables in the market but no one would buy from him. The albino in Africa also suffers from skin burn and blistering due to certain pigments lacking in the skin. Eye problems are another cause for concern. Therefore, a national organisation was formed in Tanzania to protect the rights of the albino.

At that time there was much discussion on the radio and in the newspapers about a boy who had died and was buried but reappeared again some months later. This was also one of the main topics of conversation with my students. They told the following story. A boy of about twelve years of age was found dead in his village, a funeral was arranged and he was buried by family and friends. A year later he walked into his parents house and gave the following account of his disappearance. It was said that an old woman had taken him far away to work in her house and garden. There were other boys of a similar age who were employed as slaves in the same way. The woman had certain powers which prevented the boys from escaping. One day she fell ill and this particular boy, who had been a loyal and trusting worker, said he would go to buy medicine to cure her sickness and promised to return. After many days of travelling from village to village he managed to find his way home. Villagers wondered about the boy they had buried the year before. When they opened the grave and looked into the coffin they discovered the bones of a dog. This story was believed when spoken about in radio discussions and newspaper articles and a number of other cases were mentioned where people had supposedly died, been buried, and reappeared again at a later stage.

Our six weeks of teaching practice came to an end. The teaching part of the exercise was a success. After two terms of mainly theory coming from lectures, teachers were able to use their ideas and knowledge of deaf children, to further their pupils' education. One last obstacle was the thirty-six hour train journey to Tabora, which on that occasion proved to be fairly painless. We did survive nearly seven weeks away from college but was the trip really necessary? Next to the college was the Tabora School for the Deaf, one of the largest schools for the deaf in Tanzania, with sufficient classrooms and numbers of children to accommodate all our teaching practice requirements. It seemed the obvious choice but the organisation of White Fathers which ran the school would not allow staff or students from the college to enter their building. During my two years of training the teachers I was allowed one audience of forty-five minutes with the principal, when I received a forty minutes lecture. It was all a game of politics. The principal had a dispute with the ministry of education and retaliated by isolating his school from any contact with the government college training programme taking place in the next building.

My final safari in Tanzania during those two years was to the northern game parks of Serengeti, Ngorongoro Crater, Lake Manyara and Arusha National Park. These are the most popular animal reserves for tourists visiting Tanzania. One reason for this is because they are close to the border with Kenya, which means that visitors can have a two-country safari, seeing the best parks of both Kenya and Tanzania during the one holiday. Another reason for their appeal is the plentiful wildlife to be seen, the large number and variety of animals surpassed in my opinion only by the Kruger National Park in South Africa.

British friends living in Tabora asked if I would like to join them and their teenage son for this two weeks safari. I was free at the time and would accompany them as far as Arusha, where we would have to go our separate ways. My friends would return to Tabora and I had to visit the school for the deaf in Bukoba to take part in another teaching practice.

From Tabora we travelled by Land-Rover to Mwanza on the southern shore of Lake Victoria. Roads were reasonable for travel in that direction providing it was the right time of year. We always knew when Mwanza was close by the change of landscape. Mwanza region is decorated by many huge boulders which nature has placed in some strange positions, producing both attractive and intriguing patterns. Sometimes one or even two large rocks were placed one on top of another. I used to think that the hands of two giants had played bowls or a game of marbles and then discarded their remaining toys to go off to another activity. Similar rock formations I have seen in Zimbabwe.

Another feature of this landscape is the baobab tree, perhaps the most unusual, certainly the most fascinating tree in the whole of Africa. People sometimes called it the upside down tree. So extraordinarily shaped that an Arabian legend states that the devil plucked up the baobab tree, drove its branches into the earth and left its roots stranded in the air. Its barrel-like trunk might reach a diameter of thirty feet with a maximum height of sixty feet. A strong fibre from the bark is used locally for the making of rope and cloth. It is estimated that some baobabs live for two thousand years. Local people say that when a baobab tree comes to the end of its life it explodes, leaving just tiny fragments as the only trace of a once-mighty specimen. It would not be true to say that there is a forest of these trees around Mwanza because they do not grow that way. However, their density reminded me of when I stood at the top of the highest temple in the town of Pagan in Burma and looked across the surrounding country side to see many of the four thousand temples, stupas and shrines which covered the Pagan landscape.

From Mwanza harbour we took a ferry for a thirty minutes ride across to a private guest house, situated on a small peninsula, where we enjoyed three days of relaxation. Early the next morning I walked in the well kept gardens, which had been established over thirty years before by the owner, a lady from Switzerland. She came into the garden to show me the foot prints of hippopotamuses, which had come out of the lake during the night to trample over her vegetable patch. This was a regular occurrence, she explained, one which she had never been able to solve with fences or any other harmless deterrents. Once these animals knew that succulent cabbages were on the menu, they would make their nightly visits. It was easy to guess the devastation caused by having a four-footed tank wandering at will over a garden plot. Another horticultural problem she faced on her estate was the disappearance of the fruit from her orange groves. The climate locally was suitable for the growing of citrus fruit, which should have produced a reasonable income. Unfortunately for the owner, local people were helping themselves to the fruit, also during the night, perhaps to sell to supplement their own meagre income. I was shown the house where one of the gardeners lived. A problem existed at the time of our stay due to the death of his newborn son. The father had seen an owl sitting on the house roof the night before the death. The parents now refused to live in the house and demanded new accommodation. Owls are feared because they are birds of the night, of the unknown, thought to bring bad luck to any house they happen to visit.

Every morning during my stay at the Lake Victoria guesthouse I would take the local ferry over to Mwanza and walk through the town or along the edge of the lake. The numerous rocky clusters went down to the edge of the lake, where they formed small bays which had become favourite washing areas where people took their morning or evening bath. Men and women at some time must have selected their own bathing spots, which seemed to have become reserved by custom for their own sex. I sat in one of these empty recesses one morning when three young men arrived, each carried a bar of soap, which they left on a conveniently placed flat rock by the water's edge. They each greeted me with a wave and a smile while they stripped and took a swim. I sat and watched for a while and returned more of their waves but declined their suggestions that I also stripped and joined the swim. I was afraid that if I left my clothes, binoculars, watch and money on the rocks they might disappear during my dip in the water. Instead I used the binoculars to watch some fishing boats further out in the lake. The bathers thought I had a camera, and came over to where I was sitting to investigate. I explained in sign language and my limited Swahili how to use the binoculars and let them try to sweep the horizon. Later the swimming trio collected their soap and soon turned their black bodies white for a few minutes with a thick covering of soap suds. Still clad in nothing but their coating of lather they collected their recently discarded clothes, giving them a similar all over soaping, followed by a rinse, and left on the rocks to dry. One man offered me his bar of soap and indicated I should undress and join them for a similar soaping but again I smiled and declined. Another quick swim returned the men to their original shining hue. The bathers did not have towels so were gradually sun-drying their bodies, while cavorting about on the sand indulging in some play. They asked if I would photograph them in their nakedness but I had to disappoint, due to not having a camera with me that day. Finally they dressed in their partly-dried out clothes, waved a friendly goodbye and said they would meet me in the same place the following day.

We were back in the Land-Rover the next day, travelling north close to the shores of Lake Victoria, making our way to the western entrance to Serengeti National Park. At midday we stopped for lunch, a meal I have always remembered because it gave me my first introduction to giardia, an infectious disease of the small intestine caused by a parasite and spread by contaminated food or water. Sandwiches had been provided for the day's journey, made from meat and fish left over from the previous evening's meal. I chose the fish sandwiches but eight hours later discovered I had made the wrong choice.

After entering Serengeti we had to drive to the camp site but arrived too late to assemble all the tents. Unfortunately that became a daily pattern, we would reach our destination late, it would be too dark to see our surroundings or the hotel had finished serving meals for the day, the kitchen had closed or the maid had gone off duty so bedrooms could not be properly prepared.

My first night's sleep in the small tent was interrupted by visits to the toilet at approximately two-hourly intervals. I say toilet, but it was really a case of disappearing with a lantern behind the nearest bush. I made sure it was the nearest bush because throughout the night I could hear the frequent roar of lions. I wondered what I would do if I met a lion face to face or even face to bottom when I was in my squatting position. Next morning I had an encounter with a more docile animal. Sitting at a camp table shaving I saw in my mirror an adult giraffe feeding from the top of an acacia tree, not too far behind me.

Serengeti National Park covers a huge area of 5,700 square miles, made up of a large plain with hilly ranges and isolated hills. I usually remember my visits to different game parks by one or two species of animals, either because I have seen them for the first time or because of their vast numbers. In Serengeti I saw my first spotted hyena, which has become one of my favourite African animals. Hyenas have a rather unfortunate reputation and are often described in books as cowardly scavengers. This reputation is not really justified, in fact they usually fulfil the useful function of clearing the remains of other dead animals. When hunting as a pack they will often drive lions away from their kill. Hyenas are known for their weird shrieks that sound like insane laughter, hence the common name 'laughing hyena'. My first spotted hyena was shown up in all its magnificence by the head lamps of our vehicle. It froze for a few seconds before loping off in its usual ungainly movement.

Why do we take a liking to one particular animal? I suppose there are many different answers to that question. After taking a party of children to Regent's Park Zoo in London, I asked one child which was his favourite animal. His first choice was the hippopotamus, saying that he liked it best because it was ugly and that he felt sorry for the animal. This boy was profoundly deaf and physically disabled.

Visiting a small river in Serengeti I saw my greatest gathering of crocodiles. Much of the time they stayed stretched out and motionless on the muddy banks but if an animal or man appeared within their vision they would move rapidly overland and through water to capture their victim. There is a legend which says that a crocodile will cry after eating its prey and that is why people talk about crocodile tears.

After many miles of driving through Serengeti National Park and compiling an impressive list of animals and birds spotted, we headed towards Ngorongoro Crater. Before reaching our overnight stop I was taken to a small country hospital to receive some treatment for giardia. It was an afternoon visit and still a hundred or more people were sitting about in the entrance way, waiting to be seen. Many would not reach the doctor's room that day and would have to sleep out in the hospital grounds overnight or travel home and return to hospital the next day. As usually happens when a European appears at one of these hospitals I was taken to the front of the queue and in to see the doctor. A specimen jar was provided instead of a piece of newspaper, which other patients had to use for their samples. The doctor's own private toilet was unlocked for my use, complete with water, soap and towel. Other people had to squat behind the back of the building and wipe their hands on the grass. Tests were made for me and results issued, medicine provided, money handed over and I was on my way again within half an hour. It was unfair, my being given that preferential treatment because of my race, but I did not complain.

The extinct Ngorongoro Crater, which covers an area of one hundred and two square miles, forms a part of the much larger Ngorongoro Conservation Area, with a total coverage of 3,202 square miles. The caldera, which is a large crater formed by the collapse of the central part of a volcano after eruption, reached a depth of two thousand feet, with a diameter ranging from ten to twelve miles. We followed the road which gradually wound its way down into the caldera until we arrived at its base. The impression created was that of sitting in the bottom of a huge bowl with sides reaching up to the crater's edge two thousand feet above us.

Ngorongoro Crater has a great wealth and variety of wildlife. Many fascinating meetings with animals took place. If you sit quietly in your vehicle and happen to be in the right place at the right time your camera will be clicking away or your camcorder rolling almost non-stop. My most vivid memory of big game in this conservation area was of a herd of fifty to sixty elephants, one of the so-called big five for animal watchers in African game parks. Elephants were once looked upon as fairly silent animals with little communication taking place between one elephant and another. It was then discovered that elephants communicate partly through a series of what might be called stomach rumbles. These sounds are produced at a lower frequency than can be picked up by the human ear.

One afternoon we sat in the Land-Rover close to a mud hole which, with its oozing semi-liquid mass was a temptation, we thought, to any herd of elephants. We hoped that we might see at least one elephant during our observations. Patience is the main requirement when looking for wildlife. As a child I did not have that necessary endurance. I recall my father used to take me fishing when we lived in Australia. For a few minutes I would sit with him on the bank of the Oxley Creek but would soon wander off to watch a column of sugar ants move up and down the trunk of a gum tree. A shout from my father would call my attention back to what I should have been doing, only to see another catfish carry my home-made line off down stream. My father used to say that I must have ants in my pants because I could not sit still.

After about fifteen minutes observation we spotted our first elephant making its way through the trees on our right to the mud pool on the left of the vehicle. We wondered if this was a solitary animal or part of a herd. This beautiful beast strolled majestically to within fifteen feet from where we were parked, taking little notice of us, being more concerned with lowering himself into the refreshing bath. Rolling its bulk around in the soft mud soon gave its thick skin a fine coating which would help to lessen the irritation of insects for another day. While watching this first visitor at the hole we suddenly spotted a well-grown female, with two of her offspring trotting behind, making their way in our direction. The first elephant was now leaving the pool so into the mud went the mother with her youngsters close behind. Now we had two areas of interest to watch. The first visitor had now found a handy patch of loose earth and began to gather the dust and soil with its trunk to throw over its still wet body. When this supply ran out a heavy foot would soon be used to break down another area of earth and powder it into the desired consistency. The fine coating of dust soon added another multipurpose layer which would provide a number of benefits to the elephant. It would help to prevent the skin from becoming too dry, keep the animal cool and give a further protection against insect pests. When grooming was complete each animal would turn and gradually disappear again to the right, stopping at an occasional tree to feed by breaking off a branch. It is unfortunate that elephants have such a destructive way of feeding. So often they will push over and destroy a fairly well grown tree just to take away one branch. The small Nairobi Game Park will not keep elephants because they are so harmful to the habitat. One hour after our first sighting we had counted nearly sixty different elephants, of all ages, going through the same bathing and feeding sequence. They came so close to the Land-Rover we could have opened the doors and touched them, but we had the sense not to and were more than content to capture much of the action on film. We felt extremely grateful for having been allowed to have spent that precious time in the company of those magnificent, trusting creatures.

That same evening we had one further encounter with an elephant when we were on the road leading to the hotel where we were to spend the night. Fortunately we were driving slowly because around the next bend in the road we came across a large adult male filling up most of the track. Although we were on the public highway and not in a game park, we were more than happy to let the elephant have the right of way. We gradually reversed in case the animal took fright and charged in our direction. We sat for about ten minutes, ready all the time to back again if necessary, before the elephant decided to amble off into the bush.

Later when I was back in England I thought of that roadway meeting when I heard the true story about an adventure with an elephant in a suburb of London, not an everyday happening. A man returned to his office after lunch to find an elephant sitting on the bonnet of the red mini which belonged to the head of his department. Going into his office he met his boss and casually said, "Oh, by the way, did you know there was an elephant outside in the car park sitting on the top of your car?"

The man addressed thought this was another elephant joke but went along with his secretary to look out of the window to discover that it was true. It seemed that a circus had arrived at a nearby park. One of the circus tricks this elephant performed in the ring was to sit on a red mini belonging to a circus clown. The elephant had wandered away from the park and found another red mini in the office car park and decided to take a rest and sit on it as he had been trained to do.

Not many miles from Ngorongoro Crater we came to the area known as Olduvai Gorge, made famous by the excavations carried out there by members of the Leakey family. Louis Leakey started his work in 1931, later to be joined by Mary, who was to become his wife. In more recent years their son Richard further distinguished the family name with some startling discoveries. In 1979 Mary Leakey discovered near Olduvai Gorge, three trails of fossilised hominid footprints which proved that our ancestors already walked upright three and a half million years ago. These footprints are on display in the Leakey Room in the Nairobi museum. She also found stone tools and skeletal remains of early man dating back two million years. Richard Leakey has continued these excavations and unearthed a skull of the oldest human like creature ever found. When fragments were assembled it became the skull of a creature with a fairly large brain. This member of our genus was one and a half million years older than any previously discovered skulls.

Discoveries, such as those at Olduvai Gorge, have helped to push the age of our own earth further and further back in time. Estimates as to the age of our planet have gradually changed over the centuries. The following list gives some examples:

In 1654 Archbishop James Ussher estimated that the Earth was formed at 9 a.m. 26th October, 4004 BC. I often wondered why he chose 9 a.m. and not 8 a.m. or 10 a.m. and why 26th October; perhaps it could have occurred on 25th or 27th October.

In 1869 Thomas Huxley's estimate of the age of the Earth was one hundred million years.

In 1960 Steigner's estimation was four thousand million years old.

The 1996 figure gives an estimation of fifteen thousand million years old.

My own discovery at Olduvai Gorge was a Masai warrior wearing full tribal dress who allowed me to take his photograph. Before leaving Olduvai we visited the house where Louis and Mary Leakey lived and worked for many years. This building has now been turned into a small museum.

There was one more game park on our itinerary before this safari fortnight came to an end, the Arusha National Park. On our way to Arusha we saw two teenage boys run out of a clump of bushes, close to the side of the road. These boys were wearing very little, but their faces were heavily decorated with black and white painted masks. We understood that this was part of their circumcision ritual. The East African ceremony of circumcision is quite different from the one I attended in the Northern Highlands of Papua New Guinea. Their body decoration comes from a series of cuts into the skin on the upper parts of the body forming intricate patterns which might suggest a spider's web, the rays of the sun or an abstract design.

In the Arusha National Park we saw Mount Meru, the fifth highest peak in Africa. This national park is a refuge for the black rhinoceros, which continues to be one of the main targets of the game poachers. My favourite animal seen in the Arusha park was the colobus monkey. Its slender body with long black and white hair could be seen swinging through the forest. Its contrasting coat of silky hair and long tail ending in a cluster of hair are the main features of the colobus but also at one time a danger to its continued existence. Thousands of these beautiful monkeys were slaughtered at the end of the nineteenth century to satisfy the fashion trade, with coats, dresses and shawls being made from their striking skins. One well-known tree in the park had the base of its trunk hollowed out by nature so that it was large enough for our Land-Rover to drive through. Another memory of the park was the fields of wild lupins.

It was time for us to go our separate ways. My friends had to return home to their work in Tabora and I had to make my way to Bukoba School for the Deaf to tutor my students during the forthcoming teaching practice. I travelled by bus overland most of the way, no roads existed for long stretches of the journey. From Mwanza I took a ship on the eighteen hour overnight crossing to Bukoba. The water was calm, I had a first-class cabin, so was able to gain both sleep and much-needed rest, after two weeks of bumping around on poor roads and still feeling weak after the attack of giardia. On arrival at Bukoba School I found the teaching practice had been cancelled due to the ministry of education in Dar es Salaam not having sufficient funds to finance it. I decided to stay at the school for a week with Assay and three other ex-students from the previous year's training at Tabora College. My return crossing was by the ship *Bukoba*, owned by Tanzanian Railways, which took me again to Mwanza. This time a storm made the crossing rough and Lake Victoria became as violent as I have seen many an open sea.

My two years in Tanzania came to an end and I was on my way home to England. At the airport in Dar es Salaam each departing passenger went through the customs check, which meant being taken into a cubicle by a police officer. The curtain closed behind us. The only thing the officer was interested in was money. I was asked if I had any Tanzanian currency. When I showed my Tanzanian notes these were confiscated; I had not remembered that I was not allowed to leave the country with local currency. Then I was asked to show my foreign banknotes. When the police officer started to seize these I shouted out for the whole airport to hear, "Why are you stealing my money?" It was quickly pushed back into my hands, curtains opened and I was allowed to continue without any further interruptions. I preferred the system used when departing from Malawi. When you have gone through all the airport departure channels you are presented with a form asking if you have any complaints about services or staff.

The flight into London was late to arrive and I was lucky to catch the last train of the evening between Victoria and Eastbourne.

On a cold December night I arrived at Polegate railway station still dressed in my tropical clothing, well after midnight. I was sorry to find no taxi because I had two heavy suitcases and a fine drizzle was falling. I moved in slow stages pulling one case five yards, leaving that, going back for the second one and dragging it five yards beyond the first and so the relay continued. About half an hour later I was stopped by a police patrol car and had to explain what I was doing at that early hour of the morning. I explained my predicament, received a nod in reply and the two policemen with their car disappeared into the night. I thought the East Sussex Police Force showed very little Christmas spirit that year. If they could not give me a ride I thought they could have helped with my luggage.

I have made a number of return visits to Tanzania. The first came about as the result of a letter I received from Assay, sent to the college where I was then teaching in Uganda. His opening sentence was, "Dear Brother Roy, congratulations, you are now a father. Early this morning a son has been born to the Shibanda household and we have given him the name of Roy in your honour." Later the same year I flew to Dar es Salaam with Charles to attend little Roy's christening. A custom in some East African countries is for the mother to take the name of her first-born child as her own name. No longer was Assay's wife called Margaret or Mrs Shibanda but became known to friends, relations and husband as Mama Roy. Therefore, I could say that my name was given to both mother and son.

My last visit to Tanzania was in 1994 when Charles and I took our own vehicle and drove from Kampala to the border with Tanzania and then down to Bukoba to stay for two days with Herman and his family. From Bukoba we drove around the edge of Lake Victoria to Mwanza. On then to Tabora and to an overnight stay at Sekonge. The journey from Sekonge to Mbeya was a difficult one due to the state of the roads. Three times we became bogged down in deep sand and it took Charles, Herman and myself about half an hour on each occasion to dig the vehicle free. This happened to be in one of the remote game parks, so as well as digging I kept a watch for any dangerous, hungry animal which might approach us. Charles learnt to sand drive, as we called it, on that safari. This meant moving the steering wheel quickly, from side to side, every time we drove into an area of sand. This was a desolate part of the country due to irregular rain fall and the tsetse fly. Large areas of Tanzania are infested by tsetse fly which prevents habitation by human beings or cattle.

After visiting Egha in Mbeya and Assay in Dar es Salaam we drove north to the border with Kenya. This route took us through some interesting territory. We approached the Masai tribal areas and soon had the men waving to us for a lift in the back of our small pick-up. The Masai are one of the one hundred and twenty different tribes of Tanzania but seem to be the only tribe which keeps to its traditional way of life. The young Masai boy is expected to become a cattle herder at the age of six or seven years. The Masai seldom grow crops, their wealth coming from cattle. Men have their hair plastered back with red clay. A large hole is cut into each ear with many ornaments dangling from each lobe. The favourite ear decoration that year was diamond shapes cut from tin cans. Men also wore necklaces of the same design and material. A piece of red or orange cloth hung over one shoulder and came down to the knees. Women of the tribe wore a similar costume but they did not carry the knives or spears which the men possessed. We entered a Masai village for refreshments. When a plate of meat and rice arrived there was such a large swarm of flies everywhere that I had to keep a second plate covering the meal to keep the flies out of the food.

We were driving further north when high to our right, poking out of the clouds I spotted the snowy tip of Kilimanjaro. I had made a number of visits to that area but had never seen more than a glimpse of Kilimanjaro's peak due to the almost constant cover of cloud. About an hour later I suddenly looked again to my right and saw the whole mountain from top to bottom completely cloudless in brilliant sunshine, in all its glory. I called to Charles to stop and when he had pulled off the road pointed out the wonderful sight. Mount Kilimanjaro, at a height of nearly twenty thousand feet is the highest mountain in Africa. It is a dead volcano. The peak is known as Kibo and is always covered with snow and ice. When the missionary Johannes Rebmann first saw Kilimanjaro in 1848 and made his report, most Europeans did not believe his statement that a mountain in the heart of Africa was snow covered. The people living on the mountain call it 'the House of God'. We were so pleased that our safari to Tanzania should reward us with such a fine view of Africa's greatest mountain.

Chapter Seven
Uganda – Entebbe

My first glimpse of Uganda came through the clouds over Lake Victoria, when flying between Nairobi and Entebbe. Numerous tiny islands are scattered throughout this area and perhaps the pilot or navigator is the only person on board who knows where the divide comes between these two neighbouring countries. Most of these thickly forested islands are uninhabited. One of the smaller northern islands was used for target practice by Idi Amin. He used to take groups of friends and overseas guests to watch aircraft from the Ugandan air force bomb the island as an example of how he was going to conquer the 'British Empire', as he called it. One island belonging to Tanzania was used some years ago as a detention centre where disabled people were shut away. The main group of islands in the Ugandan part of the lake is the Sese group which has a much larger population and is fairly well developed.

The word entebbe means 'a seat'. When the British administration moved its headquarters from Kampala to Entebbe at the beginning of this century, the town became the seat of government. The place where the leaders sat to administer the country. Entebbe Airport is the main entry point into Uganda for most first time visitors. This is a change from the early days of this century when Winston Churchill made the more leisurely crossing of the lake by boat to Entebbe. He was visiting as British Colonial Secretary with the task of preparing a report for the British government on the future development of the British territories in East Africa. As a result of his visit Churchill stated in parliament that Uganda was the country of the future, not Kenya. He found the Bugandan people were more intelligent, industrious and trustworthy than the people he had met in Kenya and urged the British government to concentrate on the development of Uganda. Britain brought together the four kingdoms of Buganda,

Toro, Ankole and Bunyoro to create the present day state of Uganda. The British recognised its strategic position at the source of the Nile. Entebbe became the British capital of the new country.

Sir Winston Churchill followed a long line of explorers, missionaries, traders and travellers, who visited this Pearl of Africa, as Uganda is often called, during the second half of the nineteenth century and early years of the twentieth century. He called Uganda a fairy tale with great lakes, one of the world's major rivers and snow capped mountains. The Great Rift Valley slices through Uganda, producing many lakes such as Edward, George and Albert. The Ruwensari Mountains, thought to be the fabled Mountains of the Moon, rise to heights of over sixteen thousand feet. Much of the country is a plateau between three and five thousand feet above sea level which produces cooling temperatures. Lake Victoria has an area of over twenty-six thousand square miles, which creates the impression of being a vast inland sea. It is the size of Scotland or twice the size of Belgium. Before the days of independence for the three territories bordering the lake, Kenya, Uganda and Tanganyika, the British used to take a popular three-country holiday cruise. This could begin in Kisumu in Kenya, Port Bell in Uganda or Mwanza in Tanganyika. A two week, first-class, leisurely sail would take passengers on a visit to each country before returning to their home port.

Whenever I told friends or acquaintances in England that I would soon be travelling to Uganda to begin a new project, the mention of the name Uganda always engendered the same response. Questions would be asked or statements made about Idi Amin. For example: "Isn't that where Idi Amin is president?" or "What happened to Amin, does he still live in Uganda?" Often I would be asked, "Is Amin still alive?" or perhaps someone would try to be helpful by warning me, "Be careful, Idi Amin might catch you!" The name Uganda had become associated with the exploits of Idi Amin, if you thought of one then the other automatically came to mind. Apart from the question of AIDS, the existence of Amin was the only fact most people could recall about Uganda. The legacy of Amin still lingers over the country today but it is an image most Ugandans are not proud of and one which the country is anxious to shed now that it is nearly twenty years since he fled the country. Idi Amin was undoubtedly a brutal thug and a megalomaniac but few people outside the country realise that more Ugandans were killed by Milton Obote, the dictator who both preceded Amin and later regained power for a second term of terror.

In January 1971 Major General Idi Amin became head of state, as the result of a *coup d'etat* which ousted President Milton Obote. At first some world leaders looked upon Amin as an arrogant buffoon but they soon changed their minds when they came to hear of his atrocities and torture against those who disobeyed his slightest whim. One reason the world remembers Amin and not Obote is because Amin was an extrovert by nature, a showman who played to the gallery. He took pleasure in drawing attention to himself, made statements which produced world headlines, issued threats which created fear at home and uncertainty abroad. Obote kept a lower profile internationally being content to quietly terrorise and eliminate his fellow Ugandans as a way of holding on to power. Idi Amin has established for himself a lasting place in the history of the twentieth century as a quintessential African despot.

Innumerable stories are still told about Idi Amin, by people who lived through those years of anguish from the beginning of 1971 until Amin's fall from power early in 1979. Books have been written, films made and plays produced showing some aspect of Amin's dictatorship. Some of his evil deeds are barbaric in their iniquity. There is one well-known story, which tells of the morning when Amin went off to his office but left an important bunch of keys at home. One of his wives found the keys and tried to unlock the padlocks on some of the freezers he kept in the kitchen. On opening one freezer she was sickened to find the severed heads of some of his political enemies. He would make grieving families pay for body parts of family members so that they might give them a decent burial. Towards the end of his presidency when it appeared that his rule might soon end, Amin went to seek advice from his personal witch doctor. Although he was a follower of Islam, he always kept his belief in the power of traditional medicines. The witch doctor said that a great offering was necessary if Amin wanted to keep his grip on the country. He could sacrifice either a wife or his favourite son. Amin chose his son, Moses. In a forest area, east of the capital, Amin prayed while the witch doctor cut the boy's throat. That forest between Kampala and the town of Jinja became a notorious place where people would be taken to be killed or their bodies dumped by Amin's cohorts. Many prominent Ugandans ended up being fed to crocodiles in the lake formed by the Owen Falls Dam at Jinja.

Although as many as half a million Ugandans died as a result of the atrocities performed during the Amin years of the 1970s; this figure, revolting as it is, perhaps places him in the minor league of twentieth century mass murderers. We remember Pol Pot of Cambodia, who was said to be responsible for the genocide of as many as three million of his own people during his short reign of power. We then have the super league of twentieth century butchers: Adolf Hitler; Joseph Stalin, the so-called Father of his people; and Mao Zedong.

Both Stalin in the Soviet Union and Chairman Mao of China are said to have been responsible for the slaughter of more than fifty million of their own people. It is estimated that thirty million Chinese died from starvation through Mao's mismanagement of his agricultural programme, when he concentrated on producing steel instead of allowing people to grow food. His Cultural Revolution resulted in imprisonment, torture and execution of many additional millions of Chinese. Today the people of Tibet continue to be humiliated, brutally treated and savagely put to death in an effort to wipe out their religion and culture, while Western leaders make feeble protests concerning human rights. Throughout Idi Amin's dictatorship we should remember that his main advisor was the Englishman, Bob Astles.

Some of Amin's absurd acts seem laughable in retrospect. He crowned himself national heavyweight boxing champion. Inside the ring no one would dare to be a serious contestant. If his opponent was to knock Idi Amin down, that would qualify for at least life imprisonment. The reward for a knockout would be death. On the football field he would repeatedly score goals, the opposing goalkeeper fearing for his life obliged him by allowing each ball to enter the nets. Every time the country started to run out of money Amin ordered the head of the Bank of Uganda to print more banknotes, thinking this would solve the financial crisis. One day he realised how many public service vehicles had the initials PSV printed on the back. He instructed an assistant to bring the man called PSV to his office because he must be a rich person if he owned all those vehicles. Television viewers around the world were shown Amin being carried in a sedan chair, supported by four European men. These carriers must have been well paid. A leading British politician went to Uganda to plead for the release of a British journalist being held in detention. Amin had a hut constructed with a low entrance so that the negotiator had to crawl through this hole, on his knees, to meet Amin. Another act for which Amin is well remembered is sending into exile seventy thousand Asian residents in 1972, confiscating their homes and businesses.

There is an ancient Chinese saying which states that if you want to know the master, have a look at the servants. Police and soldiers who supported this reign of terror carried out many acts of cruelty themselves. One day two policemen noticed a man walking along a street in Kampala wearing flip flops, rubber sandals. They stopped him and said that he was not correctly dressed for the capital. A gun was held to his head and he was told if he did not eat his flip flops he would be shot. The poor man of course made a meal of his footwear.

Another favourite story recounts how during the early years of his presidency Amin visited Britain and dined at Buckingham Palace with Queen Elizabeth. He is reported to have commented, "Your Majesty, you have made me very fed up with your food, when you come to visit Uganda I will make sure that you are also fed up with my food."

In 1978 some army units in southern Uganda mutinied and Amin sent troops to suppress the rebellion. Fighting spread into Tanzania, where more than one thousand square kilometres of land was captured by Amin's men. Some bombs fell on the Tanzanian town of Bukoba and citizens were evacuated from parts of the town. Julius Nyerere declared war on Uganda and Tanzanian forces, helped by Ugandan rebels, invaded Uganda. Tanzanian soldiers moved quickly through the country and captured Kampala early 1979. At that stage Amin fled into exile.

People often ask the question, "Where is Idi Amin today?" Throughout his years in power he received financial support from a number of Arab countries. Amin is said to be living in Saudi Arabia and has been there for some years as a guest of the state. His invitation from that country came about due to his deep Muslim faith and a promise not to draw attention to himself. It is reported that he can be seen today shopping in the supermarkets of Jeddah. One wonders what would happen if Idi Amin suddenly stepped off an aeroplane at Entebbe Airport as Emperor Bokassa did some years ago when he appeared at Bangui Airport in the Central African Republic.

My only contact with Idi Amin was when I was asked to give one of his sons a hearing test. The boy arrived with his mother and after an examination I found him to be severely deaf. This was after Amin's departure from Uganda. I also met the wife of Amin's confidant Bob Astles, again after the overthrow of Amin. This lady was working with the rehabilitation of physically disabled people.

In the same way that Idi Amin has become synonymous with Uganda, AIDS has also become associated in people's minds with Uganda and some of the other countries of East and Central Africa. The information which our group received on AIDS after our arrival in Kampala was very different from that given to us by the same British organisation before our departure to Tanzania three years earlier. But in that fairly short interval AIDS had become a devastating worldwide epidemic. In Uganda the veil was lifted and the facts given to the new volunteers. An evening was devoted to the subject when an International AIDS Awareness officer gave us the details which painted a gloomy future for so many people. Now a counselling service was offered, we received a plentiful supply of condoms and a list of suggested ways to enjoy safe sex.

The number of people in Uganda infected by HIV or suffering from AIDS differs from area to area. The national average is twenty per cent but some regions report a thirty per cent incidence, with other parts as high as forty per cent. The higher figures coincide with the route followed by truck drivers from Mombasa on the Kenyan coast, through the Ugandan towns situated along the main east–west roads to the borders with Rwanda and Zaire. Some Ugandans say that AIDS followed the route which Tanzanian soldiers took as they invaded and captured the country, but that predates the time when AIDS was first identified as a disease. It has been seriously stated that AIDS was unleashed by germs from Tutankhamen's tomb when the exhibition toured America. If this had been the case then why did the virus not appear at the same time in the European cities where the same exhibition was on display? Another source was supposed to have come from convicts released from an American jail after volunteering to take part in experiments with drugs which inadvertently went wrong and produced the AIDS virus, which they spread around the country. Another possible cause of AIDS has often been ascribed to monkeys in Central Africa who spread the disease to man. Whatever the cause, since it was first diagnosed in the USA in 1981, twenty-one million people worldwide have become HIV-positive and four million have died of AIDS.

Some people in Uganda have taken advantage of individual fears and the national alarm over the epidemic by announcing that they have found a cure for AIDS. For many weeks it was widely reported in newspapers and over the radio that a woman not far from the capital had discovered that soil eaten from her garden cured AIDS. This was clutched at in the same way as a drowning person clutches at a straw. Crowds flocked to her land to collect samples of soil. So great was this daily pilgrimage that one company set up a special bus service with a fleet of buses plying the route. Stalls were erected where food was sold and meals cooked and served. One trader made money by selling polythene bags for people to carry away the collected soil. This stampede continued for a month or two until people who had for weeks followed this so-called cure still died of AIDS. There was an evangelical crusade which exploited the AIDS crisis. "Fighting AIDS with the Lord's Power" was their slogan. HIV victims were persuaded by religious officials to come to be cured by a miracle. A local newspaper reported incidents of people being saved and cured of AIDS, only to find that they were still HIV-positive when tested.

Few families in Uganda have not suffered from the AIDS epidemic. Many children have been left as orphans, which is an additional shock to a nation disabled from more than twenty years of civil wars. Some Ugandans I know can count into double figures the number of relations who have died from AIDS. Whenever a cure is found the facts will still remain that an estimated thirty million people will be infected by HIV or suffering from AIDS by the end of this decade. Almost two million a year will be dying of the disease. Ninety-five per cent of all infections will be in developing countries.

Whenever I fly into Entebbe Airport I think of the incident which became known through books and films as the 'Raid on Entebbe', another of Idi Amin's blunders which brought a feeling of shame for many people throughout Africa. About a mile away from the main airport concourse is the shell of the old terminal building with the aeroplane, which was the cause of the Israeli raid on Entebbe in 1976, still standing in front of the building. The airport has now been refurbished with services to match other international airports in Africa. This streamlining means that a carousel will now bring luggage to waiting passengers, trolleys have at last been provided to help carry personal baggage and the one-time indifferent behaviour of ground staff has shown a marked improvement. The government, aware of the importance of making tourists feel welcome on arrival, has improved the standard through all stages of entry. Now a friendly welcome is usually received at health control, immigration check and customs clearance. The one convenience which has unfortunately disappeared is the row of observation windows where one could greet friends on arrival or bid a final farewell on departure. I miss the waving white handkerchief and smiling face which Charles used to present to me from these windows on my return home. Departing passengers now have the luxury of x-ray machines, duty free shops, toilets which work, a comfortable departure lounge and a cafeteria with smart dining facilities. Walking through the departure area during my mid-1996 visit I noticed that cubicles containing showers had been installed for all classes of travellers. Staff no longer seem to worry about Ugandan currency which you might still have in your pocket or purse. I could never understand the frantic hue and cry which officials made to discover any undeclared Ugandan money. I could not see why visitors would want to leave with Ugandan banknotes. They have no value in any other country. I remember one day experiencing some alarm when going through departure controls. After a thorough check through my hand luggage for currency I then underwent a body examination. The policeman's hand felt a wad of paper in the back pocket of my trousers. He asked me what I had there and I answered toilet paper. Then I was in a sweat lest he would ask to see this paper because it was in fact a collection of Ugandan banknotes. Fortunately for my future in Uganda I was waved on. I was not a visitor to the country but would be returning after a few weeks' holiday to continue my work so I required this money to pay for a taxi back to Kampala.

When booking a flight to or from Uganda passengers now have a choice of African, Middle Eastern or European airlines. My first flight to Uganda was by the Belgium state airline Sabena. This experience I never repeated after they damaged my luggage beyond repair and refused any compensation. I was so annoyed by their behaviour that I went along to the Sabena office in Kampala, to make them a present of my unusable cases. I started to book flights to Britain through Ugandan Airlines but they had the problem of not having any aeroplanes. That was not the catastrophe it might have seemed because they hired aircraft from other countries. The reason why I chose Ugandan Airlines was because they were less expensive than other carriers. I was able to pay in Ugandan currency which was convenient and they were the only airline out of Uganda which flew to my local British airport of Gatwick. Now British Airways run a popular service which also flies into Gatwick.

During a recent flight from Uganda I was sitting in the dining area enjoying a light snack when I overheard a customer ask the name of a bird portrayed in a large poster-sized photograph. This was the crested crane, national bird of Uganda. A tall, beautiful, elegant bird easily recognised by its crown which carries a golden, shimmering sheen. If the customer had taken more notice of the design of Ugandan banknotes he would have seen that he had been carrying a pocket full of crested cranes around with him throughout his Ugandan holiday. The bird forms part of the Ugandan coat of arms which is featured on every banknote. If you hold each note up to the light you will see that the water mark also shows that noble crane.

The botanical gardens in Entebbe have a peaceful setting with walks along the shores of Lake Victoria. The new group of volunteers met there for Sunday lunch at the end of their first week. After exploring the shoreline and clambering over numerous boulders strewn over one distant area of the gardens, most of us were ready for a rest and lunch under the shade of a clump of trees. One couple could not resist the cool lake water so went for a swim. This is not a good idea in any fresh water lake in Africa due to bilharzia. In most clinics and schools posters can be seen showing the cycle through which this parasite passes and how we can prevent the disease from spreading. Eggs of the parasite which live in the intestine or bladder find their way into the faeces or urine. The wall poster shows a child with bilharzia urinating into the water. On contact with fresh water, the eggs hatch, releasing larvae that swim around until they find a snail host in which they can develop further. Fork-tailed larvae later emerge from the snail into the water and upon contact with the skin drop their tails and penetrate the tissues, getting into the blood circulation, where they feed. Our clinic chart shows another child bathing in the same water and being infected by the parasite and so the chain continues. When the dangers of bilharzia were explained to our two swimmers they returned to the guest house and scrubbed their bodies with a stiff brush, soap and water. We were told that if we wished to swim in a lake to first take a boat at least fifty feet from the shore then swim from the boat. Snails like to keep close to the edge of a lake or stream. Further out in Lake Victoria they could swim free from the disease but watch must be kept for the occasional crocodile, hippopotamus or water snake. Apart from malaria, bilharzia is said to be the most serious parasitic infection. In the Entebbe gardens my special delight was to stand in the shade of some clusters of the mighty trees and watch colobus monkeys play in the branches which towered above us.

During one of our first visits to Entebbe, Charles took me to visit his mother who was terminally ill in the tuberculosis isolation unit at Entebbe General Hospital. I was saddened to see the lack of facilities provided for patients. Tuberculosis sufferers were sleeping on straw mats on the ground as no beds were available. Food was not provided by the hospitals so meals had to be cooked and brought in to patients by friends or relatives. This meant that the hospital grounds had the appearance of a large nomadic camp with fires, cooking pots, food and discarded rubbish scattered over the whole area. When a meal was about to be served, part of a banana leaf was placed on the floor at the side of the sleeping mat. Cooked food was then tipped from the pot on to the leaf and the contents scooped up and eaten from the hand.

Tuberculosis is now spreading rapidly throughout the world and is killing more people today than at any time in history, so we are told by the World Health Organisation. A recent report said that the disease would kill thirty million people worldwide over the next ten years. About ten million of these people would be in sub-Saharan Africa. Tuberculosis has already become the world's greatest killer of adults. We catch tuberculosis by inhaling the TB germ which has been coughed or sneezed into the air. Now because of the increase in population, overcrowding in our cities, the rise of HIV, which weakens the immune system, overuse of pesticides which have a similar effect on our immune system and the failure of some control programmes, tuberculosis is killing three million people each year.

When Charles and I left the isolation unit he took me to visit the house of one of his aunts. She worked as a nurse at the main Entebbe hospital and rented a house nearby. The building contained one room shared by a family of nine, mother and eight children, with ages ranging from two to about sixteen years. The room was of course overcrowded but the space was cleverly used to allow a curtained area for sleeping in bunk beds and a small sitting room. Bathing, the washing of clothes, preparing, cooking and eating of food took place outside. This arrangement saved having a separate bathroom, toilet, kitchen and dining room inside the house. It was very common in Uganda to find one family occupying a single room.

These living conditions are less frequently seen today in Western Europe but was the way of life for the majority of European families earlier this century. We think of Germany today as a rich, modern nation but living conditions in some country areas prior to the First World War were extremely primitive. I remember reading, while in Germany, a description of a typical house in a rural area. The building with its thatched roof and mud floor was shared by both people and farm animals. The room contained a large wooden bed and a smaller one, each with a mattress stuffed with straw. Two chickens perched on the end of one bed where children lay sick with scarlet fever. Chickens were running among plates and mugs on a table. Ducks helped themselves from the family cooking pot. A cow and two pigs were tethered to the legs of the second bed. In Russia before the Second World War, it was common to find four families sharing one room, a corner to each family. This situation brought about the saying, 'He did not even have a corner to call his own.' About twenty years ago I was walking along a road in a town in the north-east of England and could not believe my eyes when I saw a horse standing in a room at the front of the house. I was told that the horse lived in that room. When I saw this beast it had its head out of the window and was feeding on the grass growing in the front garden. When I remember the clean and tidy one roomed house I visited in Entebbe, where we were given a friendly welcome and entertained to lunch and remember their favourable climate, where food can be grown all the year around I think those living conditions and easygoing environment would be envied by some people in other parts of the world today.

Entebbe had a small zoo with a fair number and variety of animals housed in reasonable conditions. Now the number of creatures on display has dwindled since my first visit. One day the main national newspaper, *New Vision*, featured an article on the mysterious deaths of lions and some other large members of the cat family. An investigation took place and it was later reported by the same newspaper that some feline inhabitants of the zoo had died from starvation. It was discovered that keepers responsible for the welfare of the big cats had kept the meat to take home to feed their own families. During my first visit I took a number of photographs. Before leaving the zoo a man approached me to say that he wanted some hundreds of shillings as a fee for taking pictures of the animals. I doubted this charge because at the entrance gate there was no notice, among the general information, which mentioned a payment for photography. When I told the man to take me to where it said there was a charge for photographing animals in the zoo he soon disappeared. The most photogenic of the animals was a baby chimpanzee. He was free to waddle around the grounds and allowed us to stroke him and feed him with bananas. I have a picture in my photograph album showing the young chimp holding a banana in each hand with the caption, 'No, not another banana!'

Going to zoos, parks, circuses and fairgrounds has been a popular activity for hundreds of years. I saw an advertisement for a fair which was held at Oxford in England in the year 1642. There was a charge of fourpence for going into an enclosure to see a rhinoceros. This price compared with one shilling for being bled by leeches. Unfortunately some zoological gardens should be called animal prisons. So often we see animals shut up behind bars in small enclosures with just a concrete floor as their only comfort.

A friend in Malaysia is one of the directors of the Kuala Lumpur Zoo. He escorted me around the enclosures and later asked for my views on their collection. I complimented him and his fellow directors on the way in which some of the smaller animals were housed but asked why many larger animals, including the large cats, were kept on concrete. This he said was for greater convenience when it came to cleaning the cages. I asked why the convenience and comfort of the animals was not considered, when they had been condemned to spend the rest of their lives in those harsh, unnatural conditions. If an animal is shut away in a small enclosure there should be child safe barriers so that the animals are protected from the stones that children throw and sticks they prod through bars to wake the animal, to keep it on the move or to provoke it to fight back. I saw an example of this in the Georgetown Zoo in Guyana. Children were mentally and physically torturing animals, using them as playthings in some small enclosures where animals could not hide or escape from their tormentors.

Let us stimulate the inquisitive minds of children by having fewer zoos and more museums. I am not thinking of the old-style museums where twenty or more animals are squeezed into one glass display case. Take each animal and display it in its natural setting, say a tiger in an Indian jungle scene. Allow children to touch its skin to feel its texture, its teeth to see how strong they are and how sharp its claws. Have a series of buttons which visitors can press. One might give the sounds a tiger makes. Another could give a commentary about its way of life. A further button could operate a video showing a typical day in the life of a tiger in the wild.

An example of one type of zoo which can play an important role in the survival of an endangered species is the zoo established by Gerald Durrell in Jersey. The Jersey Wildlife Preservation Trust specialises in the breeding of rare, endangered animals and birds and when their numbers in captivity have increased, successfully return them to their place of origin. I have seen two of the projects they support in the Caribbean, on the islands of Dominica and St Vincent. Indigenous parrots are bred in captivity in the botanical gardens in Roseau and Kingstown, and later returned to the mountainous areas of those islands.

The road from Entebbe to Kampala deviates a little from the route which Winston Churchill followed at the beginning of this century. Some sights have changed little since those early years. The ubiquitous banana plants, weighed down to near breaking point with hanks of green and yellow fruit, are still seen throughout that journey. Young boys of six or seven years continue to use their sticks to stop cows from wandering into the centre of the road. Each cow, looking fierce with its wide spread of horns, seems to clear a space just in time to allow you to pass in safety. Naked children at play, women and girls carrying containers of water on their heads and men busy making mud bricks or constructing a new cattle boma. Around each house we still see a shamba where cassava, sweet potatoes, yams, beans and an occasional coffee bush grow. Frequent rain showers keep the landscape looking fresh and green with plantain eaters, hornbills and pied crows making their noisy flight from tree top to tree top. The rich reddish soil supports numerous termite hills which can rise to the height of the tallest man. The majority of houses are still made from mud bricks but now more houses have a tin roof instead of the original thatch. One great change from the days of Sir Winston's visit is the form and volume of transport now used. Ninety years ago there were no motorised vehicles on any road in Uganda. People walked great distances or used animal transport. I remember reading a report which said that Churchill rode on a bicycle from Entebbe to Kampala for an audience with the king (or kabaka) of Buganda in his palace on one of the seven hills of Kampala.

When I first made this journey between Entebbe and Kampala it was not long after President Yoweri Museveni, leader of the National Resistance army, came to power and there was still a feeling of tension in the country. At least two military road blocks would be found on this one road. In those days each car or vehicle had to stop and half a dozen soldiers would approach with guns ready for any emergency. Passengers would usually be expected to leave each vehicle and have their identity cards inspected and luggage checked. If you had forgotten your identity card then you would be detained. Soldiers and the police speak mainly Swahili and for that reason the Swahili language is not popular among the people of Uganda. They would speak their own tribal language or English, which is the official national language of Uganda. Today no road blocks exist and the journey between the two towns takes Charles an average of about forty-five minutes, depending on the time of day, to drive in our small pick-up truck. The density of traffic increases the closer you go to the capital and many accidents occur on this road but I always feel safe when Charles is driving.

Before reaching Kampala, close to the Seventh Day Adventist church, a road branches off on the right leading to Kaazi, where we find the National Scout Campsite of Uganda. This site occupies one hundred and twenty acres of grass and woodland on the shores of Lake Victoria. The scout campsite had been an army camp under Amin and Obote and when the present warden returned in 1986 to clear the site for camping once again he kept coming across bodies of victims of those regimes. When I visited Kaazi in August 1991 I met some of my scouting friends from Northumberland in the north-east of England. A party of sixty venture scouts and their leaders spent six weeks at the campsite taking part, with a number of Ugandan scouts, in a Community Aid Expedition which resulted in the building of a Leader Training Centre complete with solar power. The idea for the project started in 1988 when scout leaders in Northumberland held a series of meetings to see if this type of expedition could be undertaken. After three years of meetings, planning, a variety of fund raising activities, training weekends and necessary health briefings, the team set off for Uganda in July 1991 to join their Ugandan counterparts. A tremendous amount of dedication and hard work went into those six weeks although I am pleased to say fun accompanied the sweat and tears and new friendships were made. The project was completed on schedule and the buildings were officially opened by President Museveni at the beginning of September 1991. I recently received a copy of their project report, *Uganda 91*, which is a valuable document and an excellent guide for any group planning a similar project overseas to a developing country. It shows how an expedition has to be meticulously planned through all the stages of its development if the operation is going to be a success. I have returned to Kaazi National Scout Camp site most years since 1991 and have been pleased to meet the warden each time and to see how frequently the buildings are used for training courses and how well they have stood up to plenty of enthusiastic occupation.

I should like to close this chapter by quoting four sentences from *Uganda 91* which is headed, 'Northumberland Venture Scout Community Project':

> The fish eagle uttered its gull-like, cry as the president of Uganda, His Excellency Yoweri Museveni, opened the new training centre Kaazi, Uganda on 2nd September, 1991. The building after three years of planning, fund raising and training was completed. Every one was sad to leave Uganda and all have vowed to return. The lasting impression is of a very beautiful country with great potential, gradually realising stability for its friendly, fun-loving, dignified people.

Chapter Eight
Uganda – Kampala

The capital, Kampala, situated at an altitude of 3,905 feet, sprawls over seven hills. This area of present-day Uganda forms the traditional capital of the Kingdom of Buganda. It was selected in 1890 by Lord Lugard as the headquarters of the Imperial British East Africa Company. Lugard's fort on Old Kampala Hill, was the Ugandan Colonial administrative centre until 1905 when it was moved to Entebbe. In 1962 when Uganda gained its independence from Britain, Kampala became the national capital. The name Kampala came from the word impala. At one time the hills around the present capital were well populated with impala, so kampala in the local language meant the place to find impala.

The many hills of Kampala and the surrounding area were home to the kings of Buganda. The tradition was for a new king (or kabaka) to choose a hill and build himself a new palace. It was also customary for the earlier kings to change the site of their capital every few years during their reign. One reason for this was the need for a new supply of firewood. With the concentration of his people at the one site the area soon became deforested. Another reason for a change of location was the number of epidemic diseases which would break out from time to time. When a capital was evacuated it was usually destroyed by burning.

The Kingdom of Buganda was originally part of the much larger territory of the pastoral Chwezi people. The collapse of the Chwezi state, saw the emergence of several independent kingdoms, which included Buganda. Tradition claims that the original inhabitants of this area were half black and half white, with straight hair on the white side and frizzy hair on the black side. The founder of the kingdom is said to be Kintu, who, with his wife, were said to be the only inhabitants. The legend goes on to declare the kingdom soon became well populated due to the fact that every year Kintu's wife gave birth to four sets of twins. The boys were born with facial hair and the girls became mothers at two years of age. Kintu is said to have brought with him a cow, a goat, a sheep, a fowl, one banana shoot and a potato, each of which quickly multiplied. There were soon herds of cows, flocks of sheep and goats, chickens in plenty, while banana plantations and fields of potatoes covered the ground. We understand that Kintu's children acquired the method of making alcohol from the banana and potato, which turned them into drunken, lazy and even murderous subjects. Kintu was upset by the behaviour of his children and left the kingdom, taking with him the animals and plants which he had introduced. His family tried to discover their father's hiding place but in vain. To this day his immortality is believed in. According to Speke, nine generations later Kimera, a descendant of Kintu, gave the state its definite form. Since that time the Kingdom started to prosper.

Two of the kabakas who reigned later were Jjemba and Kalema. They have their tombs on neighbouring hills situated close to the present Hoima Road, between the small towns of Wakiso and Kakiri, about twelve miles from Kampala. Kabaka Jjemba's tomb is surrounded by a fairly modern, unimpressive looking building. The doors were locked when I visited and the guardian of the tomb was not to be found. We removed a broken branch which was used to close two wooden shutters and had a look inside this one-room mausoleum. The contents consisted of a wooden stand containing a collection of spears, which did not seem to date with the reign of Jjemba. Two pictures decorated the front of the container but these were too faded for us to see any detail from where we were standing on the outside of the building. Also present were a drum and a clay pot. The room was divided in two by the traditional curtain of bark cloth, draped from ceiling to floor.

The tombs of Kalema and his family were of more interest. We were welcomed by a gentleman who introduced himself as Prince Edward, guardian of the tombs and related to the royal family. Kalema, who was kabaka briefly towards the end of the last century, was converted to Islam by the Arab traders. When he was buried close to the present tomb, he was given a Catholic funeral. This did not please members of the Islamic faith, who said Kabaka Kalema was a Muslim and should be buried according to traditional Muslim rites, so the present tomb was constructed and is now his resting place. Nearby can be seen the graves of three wives, a brother and a son. Two of the many spears on display and a drum date from his reign, so we were told by Prince Edward. Traditional practice was for each kabaka to be buried at separate tombs which contained two shrines, one for housing the body and the other, usually some miles distant, to contain the jawbone. This was separated from his body because it was believed to contain his spirit. Possession of the jawbone was important in confirming the new kabaka's claim to the throne. This meant that the jawbone shrines gained more importance than the body shrines. Kabaka Suuna II, who reigned from 1836–1856, broke with tradition and refused to observe the old burial custom of removing the jawbone, which took place during the period of mourning. His body was buried intact. The four following kabakas followed the example set by Suuna II.

Perhaps the greatest historical attraction for tourists coming to Kampala is the site of the Kasubi Tombs, located just three kilometres west of the city. The original burial chambers were constructed in 1882 by King Mutesa I at his seventh and last palace, where he was buried in 1884. The building was slightly reduced when it was reconstructed between 1938 and 1940 by King Daudi Chwa. It is now under the care of the Department of Antiquities and Museums.

The main gateway to the royal palace is a most attractive structure built of reeds, grass and poles. This is called the bujjabukula, where guards used to stay throughout the day and night. Before going further we see a sign directing us to the visitors' building which also contains a craft shop. There we have to sign the visitors' book and hand over one thousand shillings, the 1996 entrance fee. The next building of interest is the ndoga-obukaba, where the royal drums are kept. Many traditions surround the drum which was used for almost every occasion. Also housed there is a wooden cannon copied by Bagandan craftsmen from a metal cannon introduced by one of their foreign visitors. Although it is an excellent replica of the original it could never be made to work.

The main building in the enclosure is the muzibu-azaala-mpanga, the courthouse and later burial place of Mutesa I. This impressive structure resembles giant bee hives with their roof beams of bound reeds reaching a height of about fifty feet. Shoes are taken off before entering the tomb and one immediately walks on to a floor covered with grass and woven mats. Much bark cloth is in evidence, draped from parts of the ceiling to make a screen and wrapped around each supporting roof pole. Visitors sit in the centre of the building, feet turned to the right. Facing us is a large collection of spears all with royal connections. Through the ranks of spears we see portraits of the four kabakas buried at Kasubi Tombs: Mutesa I, Mwanga I, Chwa II and Mutesa II. The portrait of Mutesa I, the kabaka with the big eyes as he was described by my guide, was said to have been drawn by the wife of H. M. Stanley, from a photograph taken of the king by her husband. Behind the portraits is an oil lamp, a gift from Queen Victoria. A third of the shrine is an area known as the forest, cut off from view by a screen of bark cloth. This is the area where the four kabakas are buried. It is not said that they died; kabakas do not die but just disappear. Very few people are allowed into this area of any tomb, but at one of the smaller shrines I was allowed to enter the forest area to view its contents, a privilege which was not even granted to the president of Uganda. Sitting to both right and left of the main entrance are the guardians of the tombs. These elderly woman are the descendants of past wives of the kings. They still attend to the dead kings and carry out necessary rituals when required. Another of their duties seems to be to produce the floor mats seen throughout the palace. The four women were all busy weaving on the day of my visit.

Other items of interest include a glass case containing a stuffed leopard. King Mutesa I had this leopard as a pet; it was tame and followed him around like a dog. After the king died the animal became wild and aggressive and killed a number of people. A council met and decided it would be better killed and stuffed for all to see in safety. Near the leopard is a large table presented by Queen Victoria. Today we can see a large television of the latest design placed on this table. I am not sure if the royal tombs are the most appropriate place for women to sit to watch the currently popular programme, *Neighbours*.

On either side of the royal palace a number of huts are to be seen. These were built for the wives of the king. During the days of Mutesa I the huts were more numerous because he had eighty-four official wives and many hundreds of women in his harem. It was also noticed by the early explorers that the king kept four young men in daily attendance for similar pleasures but this fact is not often mentioned.

For some years complaints have been made to the Department of Antiquities and Museums about the deterioration which has taken place at the Kasubi Tombs. The buildings are said to be crumbling due to neglect and several ceremonial huts attached to the tombs have collapsed. The royal palace fence made of reeds, which surrounds the site, has fallen away in some areas. Fortunately there was recently an announcement in the press which stated that extensive repairs would begin later this year.

The kabaka dynasty continues today under the British-educated King Ronald, Mutebi I, who was crowned in 1993. There has been a gap of twenty-seven years since the death of the last kabaka, Mutesa II, who died in exile in London in 1966.

Bark cloth has played an important role in the traditional life and customs of the people of Buganda. The tree from which the bark cloth is made is a type of wild fig tree. There are several species that yield the fibrous bark from which clothing, bedding, wall hangings, sacks and shrouds were made. Some bark is of a pale yellow colour, while others shade into darker hues of red and brown. Bark cloth was made throughout Uganda, primarily on a domestic basis, each house having its own bark cloth trees which individually could yield up to forty strippings. The tree was propagated by taking a branch from a mature tree and planting it vertically in the ground. Although it grows quickly, giving shade which prevents the soil beneath from drying out, the trees usually do not grow to a great size, being stunted by frequent stripping, which is begun at an early age. The younger trees give a finer and more uniform bark. After five years the trunk of the tree reaches a height of about three metres and a diameter of fifteen centimetres. The bark is then strong enough to be removed. The trunk is peeled from a height of about two metres from the ground. The soft fibrous bark is beaten out into a thin fabric by being laid on a long beam and struck with a round wooden mallet, finely grooved, giving the cloth a corrugated appearance. After the bark is stripped from the tree, the bare trunk is carefully wrapped in fresh banana leaves, firmly lashed to the trunk, to protect the stripped area from the sun. The first covering is replaced by a daub of cow dung or mud. This dries and falls away after a period of a few weeks, by which time a new layer of bark has begun to grow. The tree shows no signs of injury from the process and a new bark soon forms, which is again removed when ready.

After the bark is scraped it is sometimes steamed for an hour to make it softer and to make the cloth darker in colour. Bark cloth must not be allowed to dry out at this stage so it is wrapped in fresh banana leaves. During the beating process, which takes place alternately, from side to side, the cloth stretches to about three times its original width. If a darker colour of cloth is desired it is then left out in the sun. Bark cloth can also be left out overnight to become dampened by the dew, after which it is kneaded by hand to produce a softer cloth. Decorated bark cloth is not often seen in Buganda. For certain royal rituals decorated cloth was used. Dark patterns are produced by the use of clay or a vegetable dye. Huge amounts of bark cloth were required for royal burials. The Otter Clan held the hereditary position of bark cloth makers to the royal household. When Queen Namasole, died in 1882, King Mutesa, ordered fifty thousand bark cloths for wrapping the body and lining the huge grave. The value of those cloths in 1882 was estimated at £15,000. Today the same custom is followed by people in Buganda. When a member of the family dies the body is wrapped in bark cloth before burial.

Every kabaka received plenty of assistance from his subjects. More than fifty different clans formed the Kingdom of Buganda. Each clan had its own name and hereditary duties to perform for the kabaka. The Emboggo, Buffalo Clan, had the honour of carrying the king around during all official functions. The Ngo, Leopard Clan, was responsible for decorating the royal palace. The Ngeye, Colobus Monkey Clan, provided the thatch and built or repaired the palace roof. The Ngonge, Otter Clan, were the bark cloth makers, as we have seen, to the royal household. The Obutiko, Mushroom Clan, danced for the kabaka. The Mambe, Eel Clan, provided water transport whenever their kabaka wished to travel on the lake or river. The Fumbe, Civet Cat Clan, had a member who acted as the high court judge, and issued the truth drug to see which antagonist was to live and which to die. Another clan kept watch over the fire that burned outside the kabaka's palace throughout his reign. Other clans would be responsible for food, drink, medicine, cutting wood, bringing water, so all the Baganda people were in some way, through their clan, responsible for the welfare of their king and his family. Each clan had its own distinctive drum beat so as to know when their services were required. Most clans chose an animal as its emblem but a few were different. Emazzi-Gekisasi is the Raindrops Falling on a Thatch Roof Clan.

I was invited to be an honorary member of the Fumbe, Civet Cat Clan, and given the clan name of Ssenoga. Each year a Clan Football Competition is held at the main stadium in Kampala. The year I attended the Buffalo Clan played against my Civet Cats. I received many a handshake when fellow clan members saw my Fumbe Club badge. This was before the coronation of the present Kabaka Mutebi I. In 1991, when I saw him officiate at the opening football match, he was known as the Son of Kabaka. I saw that members of the Buffalo Clan carried him around the stadium in the traditional way.

The history of Buganda could partly be told by some of the Kampala street names which help us to remember some of the early visitors to this part of the world. Burton Street, one of the busy thoroughfares leading from Kampala Road, recalls the visits of Richard Burton to East Africa, beginning in 1856. Together with John Speke, he tried to discover the source of the Nile. The two men separated, which allowed Speke to make his choice of Lake Victoria as being the place where the River Nile made its appearance and then continued its journey north through Africa, until it flowed into the Mediterranean Sea. Burton refused to believe Speke's discovery.

Speke Road also joins Kampala Road, taking us, appropriately enough, to Nile Avenue. Speke was the first European to arrive in Buganda, the year was 1862. His aim was to be the first explorer to discover the source of the Nile. It was John Speke who gave the name Victoria to the lake, after the British queen. Speke was received by Kabaka Mutesa at his court, with both hospitality and curiosity, but one concern for the royal circle was that the explorer would not prostrate himself before Mutesa, as was the rule with all his subjects. When Speke discovered the source of the Nile he followed the river until he reached Khartoum the following year and sent a cable to London stating "The Nile is settled", but he had to wait another twenty years before his discovery was acknowledged. John Speke was so impressed by the appearance of law and order he found in Buganda that he wrote about the country and its ruler in most favourable terms.

Mackay Road runs along the side of Kampala's new taxi park. Alexander Mackay, from Scotland, was a missionary with the Church Missionary Society. He reached the court of Mutesa in 1877. He gained the king's approval by his display of practical skills, making himself useful in many ways. However, he attacked the traditional beliefs and customs of the country, making many enemies, being denounced by members of the royal court as a spy and a bringer of foreign customs. He wrote of the missionaries' fate in Buganda as "finding hatred instead of hospitality". At times he found himself almost a prisoner of Mutesa. When Kabaka Mutesa died in 1884, Mackay built in metal a European style casket for the king's body. When Mwanga was chosen to succeed his father, Mackay wrote of the new king, "None can fail to see he is fitful and fickle, and I fear, revengeful. One vice which he is addicted to is the smoking of hemp. This being so one cannot place much confidence in Mwanga's stability. Under the influence of narcotics he is capable of the wildest, unpremeditated actions." The first printing press in Uganda was assembled by Alexander Mackay. This machine arrived in Zanzibar from Europe and was then carried by porters as headloads, from the coast to the southern end of Lake Victoria, from where it was transported across the lake to Buganda. Mackay used the press to produce reading sheets and in 1887 printed his own translation of St Matthew's Gospel in Luganda. On this same press were printed some of the first stamps used in Uganda. This same printing press is now on display in the Uganda Museum in Kampala.

Hannington Road was named after Bishop Hannington, who was murdered in 1885 on the orders of Kabaka Mwanga. Unfortunately for Hannington he arrived in Buganda at the wrong time. With the coming of Mwanga in 1884, a reign of terror broke out across the territory. The kabaka gave the public executioner authorisation to kill whom he pleased without seeking the king's consent. People were burnt alive, had eyes pulled out, ears torn off, or tongue cut out. Teeth were smashed, hands and feet amputated or their genitals mutilated. Mwanga was anxious to kill and drive the missionaries out of his country. Many converts also died on orders given by the king or his prime minister. Bishop Hannington arrived from western Kenya, via the Busia route, and planned to travel through Busoga on his way to Buganda. When a local chief, loyal to Mwanga, heard of the Bishop's presence, he ordered his arrest. He was taken to a cave and placed underground. Mwanga sent the message that Hannington was to be killed. After intense torture Bishop Hannington died on 29th October, 1885. In 1986 Uganda produced a set of postage stamps to commemorate the centenary of the murder of the Christian Martyrs in 1886. The two hundred shillings stamp depicts the Martyrdom of Bishop Hannington, 1885.

Lugard Road runs in the direction of the Old Kampala Fort, where Frederick Lugard established his headquarters in 1890. Lord Lugard arrived in Buganda as the first British administrator. He quickly became involved in the politics of the area and one of his first acts was to support Buganda against Bunyoro. Lugard's objective was to weaken the Bunyoro while giving strength to Buganda. At the same time he was supporting the Protestants against the Roman Catholics. When a Protestant was murdered by a Catholic, the kabaka set the man free. Lugard stepped in demanding that the killer be severely punished. When Mwanga refused to follow Lugard's demands the British administrator armed the Protestants against the king and the Catholics. Lugard was victorious, Mwanga fled his capital and the Protestants gained greater influence in Buganda. The fort which Frederick Lugard had built on Old Kampala Hill became a museum in 1908 and remained the national museum until 1942.

Portal Street, recalls the visit of Gerald Portal to Uganda in 1892. He was sent to Kampala to report on the current situation in the country. In May 1893 he signed a treaty of protection with Kabaka Mwanga on behalf of the British government. In the same report Portal recommended the construction of a railway into Uganda. His name is also given to the town of Fort Portal in the south-west of Uganda. Lord Lugard had a series of forts constructed in the south-west to act as fortifications against attacks from Banyoro. One of these forts was Fort Portal which dates from 1893. Today all that remains of the fort that Sir Gerald Portal built in Kaborole, are the ditches which cover an area of about one hundred square metres.

Colvile Street, which runs between Kampala Road and Nile Avenue, reminds us of Colonel Colvile, who was the British Commissioner, who led the Bugandan army into Bunyoro territory in 1894. This was to teach their leader Kabarega a lesson. Colvile and the Bugandans defeated the Banyoro and Kabarega fled across the Nile into exile. As a result of Colvile's action, Bunyoro lost much land to Buganda and to the Kingdom of Toro.

Pilkington Road, also running between Kampala Road and Nile Avenue, received its name from the man who translated the Bible into Luganda. The first complete Luganda Bible was published in 1896. It was known as the biscuit-tin Bible because this edition just fitted into the old fashioned biscuit-tin which was used to protect it from white ants. The Bible was presented to Kabaka Mwanga in 1897. The

Pilkington Bible is now on display in the National Museum, in Kampala.

Port Bell Road, which takes us from Kampala to Port Bell, was named after Hesketh Bell. He was the man who carried out an extensive programme of road building during his period of administration. All available money was used to link the towns and ports in the south of Uganda by the building of all-weather roads. In 1912 he opened a sixty-one mile stretch of railway line. Large areas along the shores of Lake Victoria were infested by mosquitoes and tsetse fly. Hesketh Bell was responsible for moving large numbers of people away from this area until it could be suitably treated before rehabilitation could again take place.

Sir Apolo Kagwa Road is dedicated to the memory of the man who was katikiro (prime minister) to the young Kabaka Daudi Chwa. In 1897 Kabaka Mwanga, after an unsuccessful revolt against the British administration, fled to Tanganyika. He was exiled to the Seychelles in 1899, where he died in 1903. Mwanga's infant son Daudi Chwa was enthroned as the new kabaka. Due to the King's young age, the chiefs enjoyed a standing of unrivalled authority in the Kingdom. Foremost among the chiefs was the Katikiro Apolo Kagwa. He led a large army from Buganda to fight against the Sudanese in 1898. He took a keen interest in the growth of education throughout the kingdom and introduced modern farming methods to his people. It was Kagwa who persuaded the Bagandans to alter some of their traditional ways of life. He introduced the growing of new crops, such as cotton. He initiated reforms in the administration of the Government of Buganda. The relationship between Kagwa and the Protectorate Government was mainly friendly but under his leadership the Lukiko (Bugandan Parliament) refused to give up any of their responsibilities. Sir Apolo Kagwa remained katikiro until 1926.

The national dress for people in Buganda was bark cloth. Now it is worn by a very few high officials at important royal ceremonies, such as the coronation of the kabaka. Other places where it can be seen in general use is at the many theatres in and around Kampala, where traditional plays or festivals of music and dancing are often performed. For the last one hundred years the national costume of the Baganda people has been the kanzu for men and the gomesi for ladies. From its appearance the kanzu seems to have been copied from the costume worn by the Arab traders who frequented this area during the last century. Made of white cotton, with embroidery around the neck and down the front, the garment falls almost to the feet. The gomesi is worn in other parts of Africa. In Namibia I saw almost identical dresses being worn by ladies of the Herero tribe. Its origin appears to come from the type of dress worn towards the end of the nineteenth century by European ladies seen travelling in Africa. The style was copied and has changed little over the last one hundred years. One feature of the costume is a long, wide sash tied at the waist. Another characteristic is the way the material is gathered up to form a peak at each shoulder. The garment is worn in such a way that the hem brushes the ground as the lady walks. The gomesi is most attractive in colour and elegant in appearance and is worn for both formal occasions and as an every day dress but not for manual work around the house or in the fields.

Wherever I have lived in the suburbs of Kampala: Ntinda, Kyambogo, Masagga, Entebbe Road, or the more distant village of Kikubampanga, I have had to risk life and limb by travelling into the centre of the city and home again in a local minibus taxi. Kampala has two taxi parks, the newer of the two being slightly less congested than the old taxi park. The older park lies in a low position and when looking down upon this it gives the appearance of an intoxicated colony of ants running amok over their ant hill.

The poor state of many roads leading out from the capital is one cause of so many vehicles being involved in accidents. Another reason for frequent fatal crashes is that minibus drivers will use the roads as racetracks, trying to overtake each other at every opportunity so as to collect as many passengers' fares as possible. These vehicles are also overcrowded with conductors packing in as many people, luggage and at times chickens, as possible which brings about the situation that you do endanger your life when entering a Kampala taxi. It is not uncommon to find twenty-three passengers squeezed into a fourteen seat vehicle. Additional side seats are added to the main bus seats so that it is not possible for a passenger to move in or out of a vehicle without disturbing a number of other travellers. If a person sitting in the back seat wishes to leave the taxi then as many as six passengers might have to climb out and wait at the side of the road until this person steps out.

In addition to being squashed by your fellow passengers there is often a problem of knowing where to put your legs or feet. The floor of the bus can be cluttered with luggage which might consist of sacks of maize or rice, hanks of bananas, old car tyres, a collection of iron sheets for a roof, jerrycans containing some unknown liquid or perhaps large sufurias, a type of local saucepan, containing someone's meal, all enclosed in a large cloth. If it is a tyre then perhaps your feet will fit into the centre. The sufuria needs to be between your feet but then you are in danger of stepping on your neighbour's shoes. Sacks of food are perhaps easier to negotiate: you just have to raise your knees to almost touching your chin. The poor tied-up chickens, you have to be careful not to step on their feet or be pecked in the leg by their anxious prodding beaks. Do not be surprised if you end the journey carrying someone's baby in your arms. Try not to wear new clothes when making these journeys because you might find a pocket being torn off having accidentally caught on some piece of jutting metal or your clothes perhaps marked with grease which has coated part of your seat. Stains can be picked up from a leaking jerrycan or a sack of maize flour.

A journey, which under normal circumstances should take perhaps twenty-five minutes, might last as long as forty-five minutes due to a number of stops on the way home. Some passengers seem to use the journey to collect some forgotten items of shopping. One man might decide to buy a loaf of bread, so the driver stops and the conductor arranges the price, money is reluctantly handed over and then we have to wait until the balance is found. The same passenger might remember later on the journey that he promised his wife to bring home a kilo of meat for the evening meal. Another stop, bargaining takes place, a price which is acceptable to both sides is finally agreed, so that we can be on our way once again. The man then thinks to himself, 'I must have some milk to go with my tea,' so another stop is made to satisfy that particular passenger but remember we probably have another twenty travellers who also want to make a purchase. We must not forget the driver or conductor. Working for some hours they might decide that they want a drink or wish to find a suitable place at the side of the road to use as a toilet.

We then come to the condition of the vehicle. The taxi might be running out of fuel, need more air in a tyre or develop a puncture. Sometimes a taxi will not make the top of a hill so out climb the passengers and help to push it to the top. I remember one journey of about seven miles that resulted in my travelling in three different vehicles, the first two having broken down and been abandoned at the side of the road. Many of these vehicles would not meet international safety standards. Windows might be missing so that when it rains passengers have to hold paper or odd pieces of wood, thoughtfully provided, to keep themselves dry. You might have to hang on to the door to keep it from falling open. One hand you do need to hold on to the seat in front because you never know when the taxi will hit a pothole but the other hand might be needed to support a part of the roof which might be in danger of dropping on to you as you dip down into the next deep hole in the road. Do not be surprised if you are sitting on exposed seat springs or if the taxi suddenly propels you from your seat so that your head strikes the roof.

If you are a European and find that a full taxi has been emptied of passengers and you are told to remain and then you are asked for a fare fifteen times the normal cost, as recently happened to me, refuse to pay and leave the taxi. This could easily be a trap and the taxi crew plan to rob you once you have set out on one of the roads leading from Kampala. When you hand over your money to pay for the ride, count your change as the balance can be wrong, and look at the condition of the banknotes. Some notes might be just hanging together by a thread and would be refused by all Ugandan passengers.

When you finally reach your destination your troubles might not be over because you can be surrounded by a mass of hands and faces waiting to assist you or rob you as they so desire. Offers will be made to carry your bags, find another taxi for your onward journey or to show you the sights of Kampala. Many things you will be encouraged to buy, from a newspaper to a suit of clothes. Your eyes need to be like a chameleon's, looking in many directions at the same time. Well-practiced hands and speedy feet might soon be off through the crowd with your treasured possessions. Fortunately I have so far escaped with one torn shirt, three items of clothing spoilt by indelible stains, a cut leg and a sore head. One shoulder bag was slit open by a knife or razor blade. The greetings I receive are sometimes "Hello, Mr Whiteman", "Where are you going, Mzungu?" or the one I prefer but do not accept, "Hello my friend, can I help you?" – to which I smile and answer, "No thank you."

One day Charles met me at Entebbe Airport, on my return from England, and we had taken a minibus to the old Kampala taxi park. Walking through this always congested area, Charles was carrying one of my bags and I was walking behind with another piece of luggage. A group of taxi drivers saw us and shouted to me, "You watch that boy, he will burn a hole in your pocket."

This probably would have happened if the boy had been a stranger, but we both laughed at the warnings coming from the drivers.

Charles once said that if he became president of Uganda, one of the first acts he would carry out would be to renew the pavements of the city. A short walk around Kampala will show you what he meant. It is true that a few pavements have been remade but at least ninety per cent of the streets have footpaths which are highly dangerous to travel along. Hazards encountered would be open drains or manholes without covers, so if you were not watching almost every footstep you could soon disappear underground. If work takes place to renew water pipes, install telephone cables or repair a piece of road, then the earth which is dug up usually stays on the pavement, for you to climb over, until it is gradually washed away by heavy rain or blown away when the soil eventually turns to dust At the side of some roads there is nothing set down which could be described as a footpath. You have to climb over rocks, heaps of soil, deep ruts, as though you were following a mountain track. One footpath I have to negotiate on my way to the new taxi park has a crumbling edge with a drop of some twenty feet to water below. When a tropical storm breaks out, as they do frequently, then you have to try to find your way across an area which looks more like a boulder-strewn, fast-flowing stream. This is not a remote country town but in the capital, within sight of the Parliament Building and the main tourist hotels.

Walking around the city streets you often have to alter your route to avoid walking into, or falling over, the many sitting, squatting, sleeping beggars. Most of these disadvantaged citizens are physically disabled men. Sometimes you see a young mother, with a child in her arms or tied on her back, holding out her hand for money. Some of the deformities are the results of leprosy, with feet or hands eaten away, or a shortened, twisted leg due to polio. Some missing limbs will be the result of the many wars which have taken place during the thirty-five years since Uganda gained its independence. One morning I saw a legless beggar sitting outside an open-air restaurant where foreigners like to meet. The disabled man was watching one tourist rubbing sun tan lotion over his legs. I wonder what thoughts were going through the mind of the beggar? If you gave money to all the beggars on the streets then you would have to carry around a fortune in banknotes in your pocket. The disabled people I prefer to help are those who are doing something to help themselves, such as selling newspapers, boxes of matches, stationery items, cleaning shoes, even playing a musical instrument to entertain the passers-by. Usually I do not help those who just hold out a hand or shake a tin. Beggars assemble in areas most frequented by tourists: around the post office, near supermarkets and the smarter restaurants, and close to the larger hotels. One favourite spot is along the centre of Kampala Road, close to traffic lights, so that they can hold up a hand to the passing motorists. Recently we read in our newspapers about a physically disabled beggar who bought a piece of land last year on the outskirts of Kampala. This year he built a house for himself which cost four million shillings. Begging has proved to be a lucrative business for this man.

A different form of begging can be seen on the main thoroughfares of Kampala. You might see two or three children, ages ranging from seven to ten years, often girls, asking pedestrians for money. If you stand back and watch what is happening you will notice when a girl receives a banknote she takes it to a man nearby who is controlling this group of three beggars. He knows that being young and able-bodied, no passer-by would give him money but young girls would gain the sympathy of some people, especially the tourists.

Another form of begging in disguise seen every year in Kampala are the evangelical crusades which take place on open spaces, close to the city centre. Preachers, usually from North America, will spend a week proclaiming wonderful happenings and miraculous cures if only the audience will follow their teachings and give generously to the cause. Portraits of the preachers adorn the streets of Kampala some weeks prior to the event taking place. After three years in Uganda I was working in the Caribbean as a volunteer, renting a small house near a popular tourist beach hotel. Sometimes during the quiet season I would be invited into this hotel for an inexpensive meal. One evening I noticed a noisy couple sitting nearby with a table littered with expensive bottles of wine. I recognised the man but could not remember where I had recently seen him. Towards the end of the meal his wife came over to my table and offered me their card, saying that they were enjoying an island-hopping holiday through the Caribbean. When I saw the name I realised this was the couple who had been preaching in Uganda the year before. The money which they had collected from believing Ugandans and from followers in other developing countries, paid for their luxury Caribbean holidays. I have often been told by Africans that religion was introduced to their country by the Europeans to keep them in fear, obedience and ignorance. Europeans brought priests and educators to bind their minds and souls so that the foreigners could more easily take their land and its produce and gain their cheap labour. They speak of one big confidence trick.

Some unusual sights can often be seen when walking the streets of the capital. I used to regularly see a man whose speciality was running backwards along the main streets, somehow avoiding the heavy traffic. If he spotted a piece of litter which took his fancy he would collect this and then continue his backward run. One day I saw a man attacking car windscreens with a stick. It was said that he was anti-motor vehicles and in his confused state he wanted to destroy them.

One Saturday morning I saw a European woman locking her car when a man snatched her bag. The brave women started to chase after the thief, shouting out to people to stop him. Very quickly, as always happens in these situations, a mob of men started off in pursuit and soon apprehended the robber. He was brought back to the victim, who identified him and then the beating started, with sticks and stones, and the occasional fist and foot. Being in the centre of Kampala, police soon arrived.

I saw the man on the ground, pleading his innocence, with blood over his face and hands and on the parts of his body exposed through his torn clothing. Although the police were on the spot controlling the situation, men standing around continued to give the thief the odd hard kick when they wished.

Most days in Kampala I would see at least one man wearing just a few pieces of dirty, disintegrating cloth. This torn material would hang haphazardly over his body, exposing most parts. I have seen men dressed in two sacks and even wearing one sack hanging from the waist, probably his only possession. Just once I saw a man without clothing, walking with a cardboard box pulled up around the centre of his body. The great majority of Ugandans seen on the streets of Kampala are tidily and cleanly dressed, looking smarter on the whole than the citizens to be seen on the streets of any European town. Sometimes visitors to the country are surprised how people manage to emerge from perhaps small mud huts, in a rural area, where there is no running water or electricity, and look so clean and smart, waiting at the side of a road for transport into the capital.

Kampala now has many fine shops, a number of large markets, plenty of street stalls and people sitting along the pavements selling a variety of goods. However, there is another type of salesman who walks the streets, selling the goods he is able to carry or afford to purchase to resell. This could be a man's suit, or perhaps just a jacket he displays or a pair of trousers over one arm. Around his neck might be a collection of ties. A vendor, usually a boy, will have an open packet of cigarettes and sell one at a time. It is common to see boys with as many as four trays of hard-boiled eggs, balanced on his head, selling one with a pinch of salt. Girls more frequently have a packet of envelopes, again selling one envelope to one customer. I am still waiting to see my first loaf of sliced bread being sold slice by slice. Another lady might be trying to sell a single tube of toothpaste or a bar of soap. Some street vendors have the appearance of walking clothes horses, with their arms and bodies hanging with goods for sale: clothing for young and old, male and female; food fresh, dried and tinned; books for work, school and leisure; toiletries for all ages, and a range of electrical goods can be purchased in this way. I never buy from street hawkers, there is no fixed price and with a mzungu showing interest the starting price would be at least treble the price a Ugandan would be asked. I like to know the real price and pay that without going through the bargaining process which I know some Europeans enjoy. During a visit to a factory in Thailand I bought a tablecloth and napkin set, handing over the price they asked, thinking it was good value. Before leaving the factory the salesman came to me and returned a quarter of my money saying that he had charged too much. In a market in Malawi I bought a pair of well-carved, decorated spoons and gave the maker double the low price he asked because to me they were worth much more. Under many a tree around Kampala you can see men offering another service. A group of customers will be waiting for a haircut or a shave.

Walking around any large town you can usually find shops or buildings with names which amuse and Kampala is no exception. A place for having shoes repaired is called the 'Shoe Pub'. You can take your watch to the 'Watch Pub' for repair. Butchers have a habit of giving themselves strange names. I would happily buy my meat from

'Smart Trust Butchery' but do not think I would chance a shop called, 'Nearly Fresh Butchers'. There is a wide choice of clinics. I wondered about the 'Thirsty Clinic' and thought they might just treat people with a drink problem. I tried to work out some of the strange things which might take place in the 'Back Street Clinic'. I might be prepared to attend the 'Eye, Head and Neck Clinic' providing I had a problem in one of those areas. However, my first choice would have to be the 'Get Well Quickly Clinic'. It is doubtful if I would make any purchases at the establishment with the title 'Knackered Products'. I am sure they would not last long or already be over their sell-by date. If I went into the 'Last but First Restaurant' I might not know if I was coming or going. Perhaps my favourite name is the one given to a primary school on the outskirts of Kampala which has the title, 'Jolly and Lowly Primary School'.

In 1972 President Idi Amin made himself immediately unpopular internationally by expelling Ugandan Asians, giving the population of eighty thousand ninety days' notice to leave the country. In his introduction to the *Uganda Year Book* for 1972 he writes, "We have just ended another phase of the war which involved allocating businesses left by the departing Asians to African traders; you can now walk proudly along Kampala Road here in the capital and in other towns and find shops open, being successfully run by Africans. The African is now truly master of his own country." For the last few years it has been government policy to encourage the Asian community to return to Uganda. Although a number of ex-Asian buildings still look dejected, empty or burned out, many shops and other businesses are now once again in the hands of Asian traders. I hope this situation does not produce problems for Uganda in future. Visiting many towns in Tanzania and especially in Kenya, you can go into every shop in a street and find that each business is Asian owned. This situation I discovered brings about a feeling of resentment among the local population.

One friend in Kampala does say that Idi Amin is still good for his business. He has an antique shop and finds that tourists frequently ask for mementoes from the Amin era. Photographs, newspapers which headline one of his controversial statements or actions, sets of banknotes showing his portrait, all attract customers.

The most common scavengers among the birds to be seen around the city are the large marabou storks, grey and white in colour, standing at a height of five feet. Sometimes you are attracted to their presence when you hear their croaks or grunts which remind me of creaking doors. If a beauty competition was held for birds I am afraid the marabou would come last, certainly on my list This is due to the large bare head, heavy-looking bill, a large air-filled pouch which hangs down from the neck and a reddish-pink fleshy growth on the back of the neck. These birds are most common around rubbish dumps or feeding from skips. They also stand like tired soldiers, after a long night on sentry duty, on the crumbling facades of burnt out city buildings. They build large, untidy nests, which somehow manage to stay in the tree. The nest certainly looks uncomfortable for the fledglings which always appear in danger of falling out. Marabou storks are gregarious birds who seem to like to hop and flap around together, rattling their beaks. They do serve the useful purpose of clearing the dumps of some of the rotting food and also are an important destroyer of locusts.

Many buildings around the city centre show evidence of the war years. The two tall blocks called Crested Towers, the headquarters of the Ministry of Education, display walls and windows riddled with bullet holes. The education offices suffered in the fighting because they stand opposite Radio Uganda, always one of the first buildings to be captured in a military takeover. Whole blocks along Kampala Road remain burnt-out shells or empty bomb-sites. When Yoweri Museveni's National Resistance forces advanced into Kampala in January 1986, a battle took place on the golf course, next to Centenary Park. Guests in the nearby Fairway Hotel were able to have their breakfast on their balconies watching one of the final episodes in the takeover of Uganda by another military power. All the cinemas in Uganda stand like empty mausoleums, in memory of the days when these Asian-owned picture houses where a popular form of entertainment. With the nightly curfew which existed during the later years of Amin's dictatorship, people were not able to go out after dark and the cinemas still remain empty today. Many new buildings have appeared in Kampala in recent years which have come about as the result of money which overseas companies are now willing to invest in Uganda after a long period of stability brought about by the present leadership.

A reasonable selection of newspapers appear every day on the streets of Kampala. The most popular printed in English is the *New*

Vision, followed by *The Monitor* and *The Crusader*. Many newspapers and single news-sheets are also printed in Luganda, the main one being Bukedde. Uganda enjoys far greater press freedom than many countries in the world. Frequent articles are printed criticising or condemning the government, its policies and leaders of state, church, judiciary and the business world. This is tolerated, as it should be in a democracy. The editor of the *New Vision*, an Englishman, joined Yoweri Museveni in the bush when he was still fighting his guerrilla war. After the NRA (National Resistance Army) victory he was invited to become editor of the country's leading newspaper.

Two sections I enjoy reading in the *New Vision*, are the Reports from Parliament and the letters page. One recent parliamentary story captured the imagination of newspaper readers, and radio programmes and was the topic of conversation nation-wide for at least a week. This story was taken from a speech the vice president made in Parliament which was headed, 'Stinking Socks'. The article quoted the vice president as saying, "Some male members of Parliament inconvenience their colleagues by going to Parliament with stinking socks." She advised women to mind their bodies and to avoid the same situation. She further advised members to carry perfume and tooth brushes wherever they go.

One amusing letter from the letters page was headed, "I am looking for a wife," and continued: "I am a Ugandan aged thirty-two years looking for a young lady for marriage with the following qualities: 1. Willing to undergo an HIV test 2. Age limit eighteen to twenty-two years. 3. Be able to produce up to four children. 4. To have beautiful features. 5. Should have religious morals. 6. Minimum education two O-level passes. 7. Should always be willing to work hard and obey her husband. Interested ladies should write and send a photograph." I wonder why he did not list his own qualifications or attributes?

Uganda must be one of the few countries having no coins in circulation, just banknotes. During my early years in Uganda the one hundred shilling note was the highest denomination. Approximately fifteen of these would make one British pound. Walking into any large city bank you could see businessmen trying to deposit their money. Assistants had to be employed to carry the sacks, boxes, cases of banknotes into the building. The notes would then be piled up along the counter top giving the appearance of a brick wall growing higher and higher, waiting to be dismantled again to be counted by hand. I was once buying a car and collected around three million shillings in bundles of fifty and one hundred shilling notes, which Charles and I struggled to carry in deep travelling bags, all the way back to our college house. Today we have ten thousand shilling notes, which makes the handling and travelling with money easier and safer. Since the introduction of the Forex Exchange Bureaus five years ago, there is no problem changing foreign currency or travellers cheques. Barclays Bank in Kampala Road will pay out cash on visa cards, which are also accepted in one supermarket opposite the post office and in the duty free shop at the National Conference Centre.

Shopping has also been made easier in Kampala. The main supermarket had the system of writing down by hand each item you purchased when you arrived at the checkout. The list of figures would then be added before the money could be handed over. Your goods were then placed in a supermarket basket for you to take to another counter where the contents would be taken out once again and checked against your list of purchases. When the second checker was satisfied that the two tallied, your shopping was then placed in plastic bags for you to carry away. The whole time these transactions were taking place a security guard, with a gun at the ready, would be watching. Perhaps the threat of the gun was the reason why the frustrated line of customers did not protest their impatience and, at times, anger too openly.

Close to the centre of Kampala is a military barracks which used to be the kabaka's palace. Nearby is a lake which was for the king's exclusive use. One Sunday afternoon Charles and I had been visiting a festival of church music. On our way home Charles thought he would show me this royal lake. As we approached the area an army vehicle sped past, with the occupants indicating that we must stop, before they crossed the road in front of us. One of the soldiers entered our car and told Charles to drive back to the barracks, as we were under arrest Apparently the road to the lake was closed to public vehicles but there was no notice to indicate that the road was for military and not public use. Inside the barracks Charles was taken for interrogation while I was told to stay in the car. After what seemed a long wait, but was probably no more than fifteen minutes, I was also invited inside to join Charles and was asked a series of questions. In this situation it is better to say as little as possible, be polite, answer the questions but not to give any additional information. I had to explain my presence in the country and my movements that day. Had I used the two cameras they found in my bag to take photographs of military installations? Charles was blamed for taking a European on to a forbidden road but the officers decided that a warning was sufficient and we were released. I had made up my mind that if Charles had been detained and myself released then I would have stayed in detention with him. If the soldiers wish to be awkward they can treat local people in a rough way. Fortunately that action was not necessary. Our arrest had been observed and word passed to the British organisation which employed me. Soon after reaching our college house my friends arrived to check on the information they had received. Thankfully they found us sitting enjoying a welcome cup of tea, so preventing an embarrassing diplomatic incident.

Chapter Nine
At Home In Kampala

Living in the suburbs of Kampala during the late 1980s we used to hear rifle and machine-gun fire four or five nights every week. Sometimes the shooting would be close to our house and once I went down on to the bathroom floor in case a stray bullet came through the window. A family I knew used to sleep every night on mattresses placed on the floor in the passageway keeping themselves away from any window. At one house where Charles stayed bullets entered the room but fortunately no one was hit. To travel from the main Kampala to Jinja road to our house in Ntinda we had to pass one small army camp located under trees at the side of the road. Soldiers lived there in small structures built of grass and sticks. In addition to cooking their food and washing their clothes, they would often place a barrier across the road. This was a useful way for the soldiers to collect some extra money for an invisible fault which they used to find after a quick vehicle inspection. It was dangerous to argue with a possible bullet, especially when the soldiers had been drinking too much, so money was handed over. Pedestrians would be asked for a cigarette but if one was offered the soldiers would try to take the whole packet. Soldiers would call to me in Swahili for money or cigarettes but I would pretend not to understand, always smile, wave and say something like "Good morning" and continue my quick steps in the direction on the main road. Fortunately this seemed to amuse the men and I would hear them laugh and say "Mzungu mulatu" – "mad white man" – which left both sides fairly happy. Today I do not hear gunfire at night, rarely see a roadblock and armed soldiers do not walk the streets of Kampala.

The Ntinda house became our home for eighteen months. When we moved into the place it had not been occupied for some time, so Charles gave all cupboards and floors of the three bedrooms, two bathrooms, large through-lounge and kitchen, a good scrub. For the first few weeks our furniture consisted of beds, two chairs and a large cardboard box which served as our table. The main furniture had been ordered overseas and had to come via Kenya. All larger houses around the capital had additional rooms in the grounds which were known as the boys' quarters. We had four such rooms plus kitchen and bathroom for house staff. Although we did have a security guard living in one room when we arrived, for the remainder of our stay I kept the boys' quarters empty. All the way around the grounds we had a wall eight feet high plus two feet of barbed wire to give additional security. The owner had also planted bougainvillaea outside these walls as a further deterrent against robbers. Large metal gates with more wire on top were kept locked and bolted. I soon noticed that our security guard had his own key and would let male friends into the grounds so I never knew who would be wandering around. I felt far safer without him so asked the landlord to free us from his services. All house windows were fitted with metal bars so we felt reasonably secure. At that time we were never sure if another civil war would take place in Uganda or if rebel fighting would break out close to Kampala. The director of our volunteer organisation informed us that if there was a serious security problem in the south of the country arrangements had been made for an aircraft to land at a small local air strip to evacuate our group to Kenya.

English is the official language of Uganda but away from the capital few people have a working knowledge of their national language, especially the older generation. At one time the government considered following the example of Tanzania and making Swahili the official language but too many people disliked Swahili because it had become the language of the armed forces and the police. Luganda predominates as the language used in Kampala and the whole of Buganda, and is understood by many people throughout the south of the country. During my early days in Uganda I tried to learn Luganda and achieved a useful vocabulary of between fifty and sixty words plus many phrases. However, my young language teacher lost interest in continuing my lessons so without daily practice the initial progress started to decline. There were additional reasons I stopped speaking Luganda: my college students came from distant parts of Uganda where different tribal languages were spoken; I had problems with pronunciation; I would say a word thinking it was correct only to find

I was not being understood; a third problem was when I did use one or two words correctly, bus drivers, shopkeepers, thought I had a good command of Luganda and would answer in a stream of words which would have little or no meaning for me. Fortunately I had a Luganda speaker living with me in the new house. When someone came to the front gates to ask for work, to rent our garage or to sell some of their home-grown produce, Charles would meet them to explain, no, we did not need a house boy or girl, cook or security man, the garage was not available and no thank you, we did not require any sweet potatoes that day.

One of the most important items which make up my survival kit when travelling in tropical countries is the mosquito net. Many of the biting, stinging insects of the world; bees, wasps, hornets and mosquitoes fortunately give a warning buzz of their approach. If I am in bed and awake then I can take appropriate action: try to catch it; use a spray; dive under the bed sheet, or make sure my mosquito net is well tucked in all around the bed. When I am asleep and if I do not have the protection of net or insect repellent then the mosquito can feast on my blood. Unfortunately in addition to taking a few drops of blood it also leaves something behind, which causes the death of around two million people each year. Malaria has become the largest cause of admissions and deaths in hospitals in developing countries. This is not a new problem. Certain academics claim that malaria, which has such a weakening effect on a population, started the downfall of the ancient civilisations of Egypt, Greece and Rome. It was not until the twentieth century that scientists discovered that the bite of a mosquito caused malaria. Travellers in Uganda one hundred years ago used to say that the decaying vegetation in the ground which was brought to the surface in freshly turned soil produced malaria, and thought that the disease entered through the pores in our skin. They thought that moist soil generated more poison than dry soil. It is said that this was one reason all cultivation was left to women, even male slaves refusing to till the land. I remember as a schoolboy in England during the 1950s watching a television film which showed how malaria was being eradicated from many African countries. This was before independence when a spraying campaign took place and strictly enforced by-laws ensured that ponds and old containers were cleared and water pots kept covered. Checks were made by water inspectors and fines issued to people who failed to comply with these measures. Unfortunately after independence this programme was not maintained.

Mosquitoes are found all over the world, even in the Arctic. One world authority on malaria told me that the largest mosquitoes in the world are to be found in some Canadian forests, close to where he was born. Wherever they live mosquitoes begin their lives in water. The female lays up to four hundred eggs in any area where fresh water is found, from large ponds to an empty coconut shell containing rain water. Within a week the small larvae hatch out. Mosquitoes are smaller in warmer temperatures, so they must take more blood in order to acquire protein to produce their eggs. Only female mosquitoes bite people and suck their blood, male mosquitoes feed on plant juices. When a mosquito lands on our skin to take its meal the biting process seems very rapid so I was surprised to learn that it is a fairly complicated procedure. It is not just a matter of the female plunging its proboscis into any part of our body and sucking up the blood. The mosquito's beak has several vital parts. The palpi find the exact place to bite. Two saws operate to cut open the skin. A tube injects saliva into the blood to make it easier for the insect to suck it up. This is the liquid which infects the blood with malaria, but mosquitoes also cause yellow fever, elephantiasis and dengue fever. The experts tell us that mosquitoes do not carry AIDS from one person to another; I hope the experts are correct. If the mosquito sucks up the malaria parasites in the blood of an infected person and injects them into the next person it bites, then malaria will follow within six to fifteen days. After the mosquito bites, waves of about one hundred and fifty million parasites are breaking out of our blood cells, releasing poisons into our blood. This brings about the fevers and chills which are the characteristics of malaria. Chronic malaria often causes an enlarged spleen and anaemia. Malaria was certainly the most common cause for my students' being away from lectures. Often one can see people sitting out in the sun trying to gain extra warmth to prevent the shivering. On the three occasions when I have suffered from malaria I have piled the bed with blankets only to push them off again later, repeating this process throughout the day. A week before my departure for a country with a malaria problem I begin taking my prophylactics. The tablets stay on the table and are taken daily at breakfast time. I have been told by doctors that it is dangerous to take anti-malaria tablets for more than five years because continued use will damage vision and hearing. Before going to work in Africa I attended a health briefing and was told by a doctor that every evening before the sun goes down we should make sure we were wearing socks, long trousers and long sleeved shirts to prevent the mosquitoes from biting us. This lady did not seem to realise that mosquitoes will bite through socks and shirts with the greatest ease and even my thickest pair of trousers do not prevent them from inflicting their deadly disease.

My precious mosquito net also protects me from other creatures which might crawl over my body or attack me during the night. I am thinking of spiders, scorpions, cockroaches, ants and even snakes. As a child, growing up in Australia, I feared spiders more than snakes. Some species of spider are poisonous and more difficult to notice as they drop on to your clothing or creep into your bed. Teachers would remind us to look into our shoes before putting them on because spiders liked to hide in dark places. I stayed in one house in the Caribbean and found a scorpion under my bed. The previous tenant had been taken to hospital after being bitten by a scorpion which came into that same bed during the night. Recently Charles woke up to find a snake resting on the outside of his mosquito net. He managed to knock the creature on to the ground and quickly disposed of it before it attacked him.

The mosquito net does not really protect us against the bedbug. These small, reddish-brown insects live in furniture, cracks in walls and under carpets. They especially like beds, mattresses and the folds of mosquito nets, where they lie in wait until night time and emerge to feed on humans by sucking their blood. Bedbugs are not known to transmit any diseases but their bites disturb our sleep, cause itching and sores which may become infected. To solve these problems I would spray around the bed and inside the net a few hours before sleeping, see that the bed was away from the wall and even try to stand each bed leg in a small container of water. I never tried a remedy used by some nineteenth-century travellers in England. They would send a servant to rest in their bed for about an hour before their own bed time. This would give ample time for the bugs to satisfy their appetites by feasting on the servant's blood then allowing the master to sleep in peace, free from bites.

The household pest which I find the most loathsome is the cockroach. We used to be plagued by these insects when living in

Queensland. At night they came out of drains, wall and floor cracks and other favourite dark places, in their quest for food. The most unexpected things would be eaten: eyelashes from a child's doll; part of an umbrella left out overnight to dry; pages and bindings of an open book; a hole would be discovered in a favourite pair of trousers. They did, of course, eat nearly all forms of uncovered food: a meal left out for the cat; seed in the parrot's cage; vegetables in a box; fruit in a basket. They could eat their way into packets in the cupboard. I shudder at the obnoxious sight I remember in Tanzania of a large cockroach sitting on the bristles of a toothbrush, presumably sucking up the residue of moisture. Now I always use a traveller's toothbrush which comes enclosed in a plastic case. Cockroaches generally give off an unpleasant smell. They spread disease and are a menace to public health especially when found in kitchens, restaurants, bakeries and hospitals. I once bought a tin of jam in England and on opening the tin found three inches of adult cockroach inside. These insects therefore are not confined to tropical countries. I have seen many in England, especially when working in older buildings. Cockroaches are survivors and were among the earliest forms of insect life appearing during the Coal Age. Fossil remains show they have changed little since those early times millions of years ago. These hardy creatures can survive even in extreme temperatures. Reports state that a cockroach recovered after being frozen in liquid, regaining mobility once it was restored to room temperature. Another example spoke of a cockroach walking out of a microwave oven after having been baked for three minutes. In one African house I would visit the pit latrine every evening after dark and find thirty to forty fully grown cockroaches crawling over the walls and floor. Toilets are one of their favourite areas. When men have been placed in prison camps and food has been scarce cockroaches were said to have been scraped from the walls of the latrines in large numbers, cooked and eaten for their high protein value. Prisoners near to starvation would catch cockroaches to eat alive. Just the thought of this is most repulsive but so far I have not found myself in such a desperate situation so I cannot say that it would be an impossible act for me to carry out. However, I am sure I would be so nauseated that I would gain little from its food value. The only good thing I can say about this insect is that it kills and eats bedbugs but even that service does not make the cockroach any more endearing to me.

On a happier note our first house in Kampala had a large garden which contained many banana plants. This was my first experience of having my own bananas growing outside the kitchen door. Every day I would watch for signs of the fruit developing. When flowers appeared and I noticed the first slim fingers of bananas my interest increased. Charles told me that I had to be patient because it might be another three to four months before the crop would be ready for eating. Eventually the bunch changed from green to yellow and the size looked suitable for plucking but again Charles said to be patient because another three weeks of waiting was necessary. Finally the morning arrived when Charles announced that we could cut and eat our first home-grown bananas. To my horror I saw him take a machete and hack away at the trunk of the plant. I shouted to Charles to stop because I wanted to keep this tree so that we could have a second crop. In my ignorance I did not understand how bananas reproduced. Charles explained that the banana is not a tree but a plant and its life is perpetuated by sending out numerous suckers. The main trunk is cut down and new plants will grow in its place. Although some species of banana reach a height of over twenty feet, no wood is formed: it is a stem which is formed by tightly growing leaves which fold within each other to produce this false trunk. The banana plant often becomes top heavy when it has a weighty hank of fruit to support. Plants will be found leaning at odd angles precariously supported by crooked stakes. The banana is a wonderful food item, containing a collection of seven different vitamins all cleanly wrapped in a skin which needs just the slight effort of peeling before we can enjoy a nourishing meal. Bananas are easily digested and a good source of energy, being rich in carbohydrates and sugars. One heavy hank contains many individual bananas which soon filled our kitchen table and shelves with fruit. We could eat perhaps four of five a day, so friends and neighbours also benefited from our crop. Charles told me that there are as many as sixteen different varieties of banana in Uganda. They vary in colour, size of fruit and degree of sweetness. Some bananas are for boiling before eating, others for roasting and one variety is used for making a local drink. I can never tell one banana plant from another by looking at the plant. To me a banana is a banana, but Charles knows by the look of the leaves which variety we had growing in the garden.

So rapidly does vegetation grow in Uganda that the explorer H. M. Stanley described Uganda as being "a land that knows no Sabbath". The land never seems to rest and keeps producing. People say that you just have to plant a seed and sit back and wait until it is time to pick the fruit. Some crops of course take longer to grow to fruition than others. If you are going to live in a country for twelve months or less, some food plants would not be worth growing if you wish to use the fruit for personal consumption. One quick growing plant, an attractive addition to the garden and a pleasant nutritious fruit to eat, is the pawpaw. This popular tropical fruit tree grows in most hot and humid parts of the world. There are forty-five different varieties of pawpaw, with variations in colour, size and taste of fruit and size of tree. Some trees can reach a height of thirty feet. There are separate male and female trees which require the aid of insects for pollination. In our present garden we have at least twenty pawpaw trees. Although it is classified as a tree, the pawpaw does not possess the usual wood of a normal tree. The trunk is fibrous and is often hollow, which sometimes brings it crashing to the ground in a storm. The benefit of this tree for the short-stay visitor is that it can produce fruit in just five to six months from planting the seeds. Some pawpaw are huge and can attain a weight of ten pounds. The fruit is orange to yellow in colour and when ripe is often eaten with a squeeze of lime or lemon. My father used to slice the pawpaw in two, scrape out the hundreds of black seeds and fill the space with ice cream. The two halves were then placed together and returned to the refrigerator and eaten as a welcome dessert. Pawpaw will cure constipation but just a word of warning: too much of the fruit will bring about the opposite condition.

My work in Uganda was at the Special Education Department, Kyambogo College, where I trained teachers to work with disabled children, who were either deaf, mentally disabled or physically handicapped. The walk from our Ntinda house to college took forty-five minutes in each direction. I had two choices of route: through the swamp or along the main Kampala to Jinja Road. I preferred the peace and quiet of the cross-country walk to the noise and pollution of the traffic. A valley separated Ntinda from Kyambogo with a stream at the bottom which divided the swamp. During the dry season it was a fairly easy walk along the path, which would in parts fluctuate with each step, through the swamp, where villagers would squelch about in the mud, planting, tending or harvesting their crop of yams. Across the stream were two tree trunks which I successfully negotiated each day, gingerly stepping on to the logs, balancing with outstretched arms across the centre, going into a slight run as I reached the end and finally jumping on to the safety of the far bank. Every day I approached this bridge with some trepidation because one of my colleagues took a tumble and ended up in the water. Throughout this valley walk to college I was entertained by colourful, musical birds and the meandering flight of butterflies, which are usually large and beautiful in tropical countries. Children were running to school and adults walking, pushing bicycles or carrying some agricultural produce, gathered from the swamps or valley edges, balanced on their heads. College staff warned me not to use the country walk every day. They had the fear that I might have been ambushed and robbed, which could have happened. Once or twice a week I faced the traffic along the Jinja Road. It was not usual to see a European walking; they had cars and did not walk out in the heat of the day. My field director promised me a Land-Rover but this never materialised, so for eighteen months I walked or, as Charles used to say, I went on shanks' pony.

One morning, on entering college grounds, I saw a mass of soldiers, military transport and a great quantity of weapons. Armed soldiers stood around in small groups, others were lying under trees and in ditches supporting grenade-launchers and two trucks were packed with soldiers and bristling with sub-machine guns. Had a *coup d'état* taken place, I wondered? As I entered the college gates two soldiers motioned with their machine guns that I move towards a tree. I was then instructed to stand under the tree without any explanation as to what was happening. A few minutes later this whole area came to life, soldiers ran, trucks moved, guns were held ready to fire, soldiers manning the grenade-launchers tensed themselves for action, a convey formed and started to roll forward towards the main exit. As I watched the centre of the hubbub I saw a Mercedes-Benz flying the presidential flag and spotted the President Yoweri Museveni, sitting in the back. His Excellency had been addressing a gathering of students and staff in the auditorium that morning. About a year later, when I was living at the college, I had a similar presidential encounter. I walked from the college house to my office, a journey which took one minute, when I met a ring of soldiers around the main administrative buildings. I was stopped and told that if I wanted to go to my office I would have to undergo a body search plus my document case had to be emptied out on to the grass. The reason for this inspection was because the president was going to make another visit to the college that morning. I refused to have a body search to enter my office so I told the soldiers I would return to my house and work from there for the rest of the day.

Soon after I arrived in Uganda and started to lecture at college I was told that my stay in the Ntinda house would be temporary, as a new house was being built for me at Kyambogo. The building of this chalet-style bungalow started, but delay after delay took place and promised completion dates given by the Kenyan-based construction company would come and go. Finally, after one and a half years, the house was said to be ready for occupation, all work had been completed and keys handed over. When Charles and I arrived with our bags and furniture I was more than a little chagrined to find that a layer of liquid mud covered all the floors. We tried to hide our months of frustration and cleaned out the bungalow as quickly as possible so we could sleep there that night. We soon found that the builders needed to make a return visit to our new home. When constructing the bathroom they had made the floor slope in the wrong direction. Instead of water from the shower running away down the drain, it ran through the house flooding bedrooms and lounge. I was happy to be living at the college because it meant that my walk of forty-five minutes from Ntinda to Kyambogo changed to a walk of one minute from house to office and lecture room.

Soon after moving into the Kyambogo house Charles' half sister Norwa came to live with us. We found a place for her at the local primary school where she entered the first class. One morning she ran off to school but quickly returned home to ask me for an empty jam jar, explaining that this was to catch termites which had been swarming around a nearby street lamp. From the kitchen window I could see a small group of excited infants collecting handfuls of these edible insects. We were experiencing what is known in the insect world as marriage flight. From time to time swarms of flying termites suddenly leave their different nests at the same time and take to the air. This makes it possible for males and females, the future kings and queens of termite society, to come together to mate. The royal couples which escape being caught and eaten by birds, lizards or eager children, shed their wings and burrow into the ground to create a small space in which the new queen starts to lay eggs. She really turns into an egg-laying machine with some species laying one egg every second, every minute, hour, day, for as many as ten years. When we add this up we find that she is capable of laying three thousand six hundred eggs each hour, over eighty-six thousand per day, six hundred thousand plus in one week and over thirty million a year. If the queen lives a full lifespan this would mean that each of those swarming females I watched from my kitchen window could produce an incredible three hundred million new termites. It is not surprising that more termites are thought to exist than any other insect. However, they are rarely seen because termites spend most of their lives living underground or above ground in their mounds of hard earth which can rise as high as twenty feet. The termites' nest reminds me of an iceberg because there is more of it existing underground than above ground. Deep within the nest the indulgent queen is being stuffed with food by her dutiful servants. A continuous chain of nurses carry away the eggs, coating them with a saline solution which prevent the growth of mould, before each egg is deposited in the hatchery. A central heating system exists so that the nursery is kept warm. This is provided by amounts of fermenting vegetation which has been collected by the workers. Some colonies establish gardens where termites grow mushrooms and even keep 'cows' for milk. Cows in the termite world are small beetles, found only in termite colonies, which secrete a liquid which the termites enjoy drinking. Different termites have different tasks to perform within the nest When a new colony is established the eggs produced by the queen hatch out as blind and wingless workers which have the task of enlarging the nest Termites dislike light, so when there is a need for them to work above ground they will construct covered runways to protect themselves from daylight. When soldier termites are produced they have the work of guarding the colony and searching for food and water. Norwa did not realise that every pair of male and female termites she caught and enjoyed eating during her mid-morning school break could have established a colony of workers, soldiers, farms, nurseries, all revolving around a queen, capable of producing as many as three hundred million new termites in her lifetime.

When Norwa attended school for the first time I gave her a new pencil and exercise book. The pencil was placed inside the book and both were placed on the head and off she walked to join her friends and classmates. Looking over the garden hedge one could see a line of schoolbooks and an occasional lunch box moving along the track leading to the classrooms. Norwa would return from the village shop after buying a carton of milk, a tin of jam or a loaf of bread, with these items never carried in the hand; everything always went up on to the head, it became an automatic action for all children. I never ceased to be amazed by what could be balanced and supported by the head: a hoe being taken to dig in the shamba, a hank of bananas to sell in the market, a heavy branch carried home to be chopped up for firewood. I always have a struggle when I try to carry a twenty-litre jerrycan of water back from the well. A lady would overtake me with one full jerrycan in the hand and a second can on the head. Often I have departed from a house and had my bag taken from me by a friend to be carried on her head to the bus stop. If a visitor carries his own bag from a house it means that he will not return. One of the few things I have not seen travelling on top of the head is a baby, which is always carried on the back. When visiting a market in Kano, northern Nigeria, I saw a young lady balancing a tray with about thirty eggs on top of a cloth which covered her head. She saw something on the ground, stooped to pick it up and continued on her way, never once touching the tray with a hand, and showing perfect balance. When working with children in England I have played the game of walking with a tin can or plastic plate balanced on the head but so often children have failed and the tin or plate soon clattered to the ground. This skill had been too difficult to maintain. I know that British children have not practised this task in the same way as the African child but European children do not seem to have the same natural poise and deportment which comes so naturally to Norwa and her friends in Africa.

The next resident to arrive at the Kyambogo house was Tommy, named after our friend Violet's cat in England. Perhaps Tammy would have been a more appropriate name, because after a few months she gave birth to three kittens. Tommy was an affectionate cat and a caring mother. One morning I placed a dish of meat on the front porch for both Tommy and the kittens, which were now eating independently. I noticed a strange piece of behaviour which I had never seen before or read about. Tommy took a piece of meat, carried it a few yards to the garden, dug a hole and buried it. I wondered if she wanted to save this morsel from being eaten by the kittens, a small snack she could enjoy at a more peaceful period of the day. I am used to dogs burying food, but not cats. When I was staying in a friend's house in Thailand, one of my shoes was taken by her dog and buried somewhere in her large garden. We played hunt the thimble for hours before my shoe was discovered. At least the garden looked generally fresher after our digging. Norwa enjoyed playing with Tommy, which would never tire of chasing a piece of cloth tied to the end of a string. Before returning to Uganda after a holiday in England, my friend Violet gave me box of cat biscuits. We would give Tommy a few each day but she always looked for more. No matter where in the house I put the box Tommy would discover its hiding place. Cupboard doors would be pawed open, drawers and contents clawed out, she would find a way to climb to the top of our wardrobe and knock the box to the ground and eat some of the contents before we reacted to the noise. I should have experimented and buried the box in the garden and watched to see if she located it, dug up the box and ate its contents.

A study of animal behaviour is often a useful way of discovering and understanding more about how humans behave. I am grateful to my friend Shaul Penn, who lives and works at a kibbutz in Yizreel, Israel. Shaul wrote the following account of his experiences when working with cows suffering from blindness:

> Over the last twenty odd years I have had about three to four cases a year of blind calves and while most other breeders would tend to send them to an early slaughter I have battled it out with them and in the majority of cases the males have lived their normal year or so before moving on and most of the females have become cows in our dairy or sold to other dairies. At first the blind calf finds it impossible to cope with getting to the artificial teat and to the water and feed bins, so I have to enter and physically move her from one to the other in order to train her. By doing this she suffers the jealousy of the other calves in the group (normally eight to twelve in a group) and they head-butt her and try to keep her away from the food. So what I have learned to do is train one or two normal calves at the same time and this has solved the

problem. Later, every time the blind calf moves to another area of the cowshed I again need two or three days to show her around. When the calf becomes a cow nobody can tell the difference and as a cow the three times a day walk from cowshed to milking parlour and back and finding the food and water is no problem at all. In fact most of my fellow workers in the milking parlour do not even know that some of the cows that they are milking are blind, and even when they change them around to different cow sheds their sense of smell and hearing are such that they have no problems.

Shaul goes on to say:

Next year I will undertake a study of twin calves. If the twins are male or female, in over ninety per cent of cases the male gets most of the hormones and the female is infertile. In the case of two females they are normally small and nobody really knows if they are worth holding on to or not. This is what I want to research.

Not long after Tommy's arrival we acquired two goats. This was the result of a visit to Pallisa in eastern Uganda, where I visited a special unit for disabled children established by Vincent Oken, one of my ex-students. Charles and I stayed overnight in the family house but due to an earlier stomach upset I was not able to enjoy much of the family meal. The fact that I ate very little food disappointed Vincent so to compensate for the meagre amount I consumed in his house he presented me with a healthy female goat. On our departure from Vincent's village the goat was placed in the boot of our car and off we went on the homeward journey to Kampala. When we reached the town of Pallisa and saw a market, Charles thought it would be a good idea to buy another goat as a companion so we purchased a male to join her in the boot. Jack and Jill, as we called the pair, arrived back at college and soon recovered from their journey. We provided a shelter for them to spend each night and tethered the goats just as the sun was setting. About a week later I discovered both goats were free from their ropes. For the next half an hour I tried to catch them by getting close enough to clasp my arms around the necks of Jack or Jill, but ended up with a small tuft of hair each time or lost my footing and stumbled over in an area of long grass. They both managed to avoid capture so I gave up and retired to read on the porch. Later that evening I found them both sitting happily under their night-time shelter, so we never tied them again overnight; they had accepted their nightly resting place and were happy to use the shelter we had provided.

The giving of an animal as a gift when I visited a Ugandan friend was very common but the present was usually a chicken. The first time this happened I was presented with a squawking, wings flapping, agitated hen. Thinking of my long return journey to the capital, which included walking, a ride on the back of a bicycle and two different buses, I asked if I could change my bird for some eggs. This idea was quickly rejected and I was told that my chicken would be wrapped in newspaper, the bundle carefully tied with string and I would have no further problems. Also I should think of the chicken meal which my gift would soon provide. I explained that I would not eat my new hen but would keep and feed her as a family pet. This was looked upon as rather strange but as she was now my chicken I could choose what I did with her. Home again with Chook, the name I selected for our new pet, every day I was pleased to see her roaming around the garden. It took some time to stop Tommy chasing Chook and trying to give her flying lessons around every tree and bush. Why, I wondered, could Tommy not behave more like Jack and Jill and ignore poor Chook? One Saturday morning before going off to town I started to give the chicken her usual food. Charles tried to tell me not to feed her that day but I could not think of a good reason why she should go without her breakfast. Arriving home later the same morning I could not find Chook but noticed that we had unexpected chicken on the luncheon menu. I went without lunch that day and was sorry that I never had to provide Chook with another breakfast.

It was no surprise to see grasshoppers jumping about in the fields, a sight to be seen in most countries, but I had not seen them on sale before in the market as an item of food.

Among the fruit and vegetables in the main Kampala market I saw polythene bags with green objects jumping about inside. Charles said that these were grasshoppers being sold, they were good to eat and could we buy some to take home to cook for our evening meal? The price was rather high so we bought just the one bag which contained about twenty insects. That evening Charles was busy cooking our meal which included the newly purchased grasshoppers. I did not ask, or want to know, how he prepared and cooked these creatures. One thing I could see when the plate was on the table was that somewhere in the process they had lost their legs. I waited without any real desire to taste the grasshoppers and hoped that Charles would forget to offer me one. The plate was eventually passed, as I knew it would be, and I consumed three or four shrunken, green bodies, in the same way one would eat a shrimp. The taste was also shrimp-like, but of a more crunchy texture. I later discovered that grasshoppers provide a more nourishing meal and have a protein value higher than meat, chicken or fish.

Being resident at college meant that I now saw and spoke with many more students also living as members of a large college community. We would meet at the college shop or in the library, when walking to the bus stop or waiting for transport. Names would be exchanged and I became intrigued by the variety of names chosen. The unusual choice of first name used to interest me. Sometimes a day of the week was taken so I would be walking along with Thursday, Friday or perhaps a Saturday. I was fairly sure of the day of birth of one young lady who introduced herself as Easter Monday. In one group were to be found students with the names of Aphrodite and Romeo. I wonder if that young man and woman became friends? In East Africa some names have a patriotic meaning: Uhuru (freedom), Taifa (national), Kenya (country of birth). Other names might have a pleasant or even unpleasant association: Furaha (joy), Baraka (one waited for). I met an unfortunate deaf boy at Buguruni School in Dar es Salaam, who had been given a name by his parents which meant 'we wish you had never been born'. I was amused during a recent sojourn in the Caribbean where I met one family with three sons whose names were, Nylon, Rayon and Polyester. Another mother on the same island was going to name her daughter Tampon, because she liked the sound of the name. Fortunately for the sake of the child the mother was persuaded to choose an alternative name. In the Caribbean we find many people have the same surname on the one island. This dates back to when the slaves arrived from Africa and were given Christian first names and their master's surname. All the slaves working on one plantation would have the same last name: Morgan, Campbell, Richardson, O'Conner. In Uganda, men of the Karamojong tribe, who are cattle-keepers, are often named after their favourite cow. It would be like a man in England being given the first name of Buttercup. Some tribes do not choose any name for a daughter but look upon her as a visitor who will remain in their household for the first twelve or so years of her life until she goes to join her future husband and will then become a member of his family.

One tradition I did not realise before going to East Africa is that you do not write to someone using a red pen, unless you are writing to inform them that a person has died. One evening at college I started to write a letter to one of my ex-students when my usual pen ran out of ink. The only other pen available in the house had red ink so, without understanding the consequences, I used that pen. I received a quick reply from Friend Moses to say that on receiving my letter he went into a state of mild shock waiting to find out which of his friends or relations had died. When he read my friendly greetings he felt that he had to answer quickly to explain the use of the red pen in Africa, as an instrument which announces death, before I wrote any more letters using this colour. Red is generally thought of as an unlucky colour associated with blood, injury, bad luck and death. In the same way some people in England think of green as being an unlucky colour and would never buy or wear it. When my mother died two years ago I wrote to Charles from England to announce the sad news, writing with a red pen. As soon as he saw the colour of the writing on the envelope he knew that the end had arrived. Charles had been in England with my mother just a few weeks before she died.

When abroad some people are content to immerse themselves in local news and events, happy to forget what is happening in the rest of the world. This might be a welcome relief if you are overseas for a week or two, taking a well-earned holiday and wish to relax and recuperate, perhaps on a small island, free from the anxieties you left behind in your own troubled country. However, when living away from home for a longer period of time I am not satisfied with local news and gossip, which I can easily pick up free if I wish from friends and colleagues. Without access to international news I would not know if I woke up one morning and half the world no longer existed and I was isolated for the rest of time on my small tropical island with a population of twelve hundred inhabitants. Some countries are more insular than others when it comes to what is reported over the radio or television and printed in newspapers. Often this is a situation which the government has forced upon the media and not one of their own choosing. I can think of some African countries where the first news item on radio or television is always something about their president, however trivial that story might be. I am sure that if there was a major international disaster, these countries would still find something to say first about their president. The news bulletin might begin as follows: "This morning the president had his cup of coffee and two slices of toast before setting off to go to his office. During the night there was a gigantic explosion in the Pacific area and Australia disappeared under the sea. So far no survivors have been found."

When living in Kampala my main lifeline to the outside world is a nightly attempt to listen to the BBC World Service. Until I pressed that vital switch, which I hoped would bring me the chimes of Big Ben, I never knew if I would receive the eagerly awaited news or a cacophony of sounds which ranged from a skylark singing to a billion bats breaking out of bedlam. Why, I wonder, do I always experience more difficulty when I want to tune in and gain a clear reception from the BBC than from any other station I try? If I wished to listen to Voice of America, broadcasts from France, Germany, or news from South Africa, I could sit back and enjoy half an hour of uninterrupted pleasure. Why do I have such a struggle to pick up my favourite programmes from London? My expensive digital radio would often give me the voice of a middle-aged Italian soprano singing an operatic aria or what sounded like a troop of Lancashire clog dancers performing on a hollow wooden platform in an empty church hall. In frustration I would switch off and hope to catch the report of Alistair Cooke's *Letter From America* later that evening.

Sometimes my radio, with its additional aerial looped around the room, plus individual ear pads, which are supposed to give a clearer reception, would allow me to catch some key words which I had to try to make into a plausible story. Perhaps I picked up "White House", "George Bush" and "Vietnam". Then I had to decide if the information meant that ex-President Bush had made a visit to the White House to brief President Clinton on a recent visit to Asia, or if White House officials had appointed George Bush to head a trade or peace delegation on a coming visit to Hanoi. I have encountered the same difficulties in four continents with three different radios when trying to find the correct wavelength for the BBC service. Occasionally I would have a treat, with reception being so loud that I could work in the kitchen or bedroom and still clearly hear all that was coming from the radio on the dining-room table. Then I knew the value of the pound against the dollar; what the British newspapers had to say, and could enjoy John Tidmarsh and his friends presenting *Outlook* or Ian Anderson keeping us entertained each week with *Folk Routes*. I once heard a letter from a listener who asked the BBC to explain the final item of a recent news bulletin which ended with the words "fish and chips". The presenter of this feedback programme was able to discover a recording of that news and we heard the final sentence again, which ended with the words "efficient ships". Twice over the last year I have had a similar experience and just caught the final parts of two sentences and wondered what they were about. One ended with the words "for urine drinkers". The second announcement some weeks later stated that "the best product for those in love with incontinence". Did I hear correctly, or were the words I thought I heard actually something quite different?

Another source of enlightenment when overseas is the airmail edition of the *Guardian Weekly*. This has been a constant companion for the last twelve years, apart from the time when post office staff, especially in Tanzania, borrowed my copies and forgot to send them on their way again. I hope they also enjoyed a good read and gained as much pleasure from its pages as I do. Due to postal delays my copy of this newspaper often arrived a few weeks after publication which meant that news items were out of date. The threatened strike, election result, or an eagerly awaited state visit had now passed into the history books. For this reason I do spend more time reading through the leisure section than items of current affairs which I hope to gain from my radio. For many years I have been entertained by Ralph Whitlock's weekly column. Sadly, he is no longer able to share his great knowledge of wildlife with *Guardian* readers. Ralph has kept records from personal observations over many decades with additional information coming from a large band of followers from many different parts of the world, which he shared with us. When he wanted to discover the source of some tradition or the way our forefathers used to live, he would walk to the bottom of his garden to consult with his ancient relative who was born around the middle of the last century. Sometimes I managed to complete the *Guardian* crossword puzzle, the quick one I hasten to add. The cryptic crossword is always beyond me; I never achieve more than half a dozen correct answers and that is during a good week. I enjoy reading 'A Country Diary', my favourite contributor being Veronica Heath writing about the beautiful county of Northumberland. I am fascinated by the long letters which appear in the leisure pages from readers in different parts of the world, perhaps Senegal or Madagascar, explaining traditions, customs, taboos, in their country. The book section gives an excellent review of new titles which helps me to add to my ever-growing list of books which I hope to read one day. Some countries where I have lived in recent years, Nevis Island, Anguilla, Uganda, have no cinemas but I still make a note of films I should like to see from the paper's weekly reports. Most of the films I now watch come by courtesy of British Airways in-flight service. The sports pages also keep me in contact with achievements which have taken place over recent weeks. As the season progresses I can find out if Oxford has managed to win the University Boat Race. Was Damon Hill still leading in the motor racing championship? How Arsenal were faring in the football Premiership. Did Michael Atherton score a century in the test match and lead England to another victory? Would Boris Becker reach the Wimbledon final once again? The progress which Middlesex was making in its bid to win the County Championship title for another season. Long may the *Guardian Weekly* keep appearing in my post box each week.

Chapter Ten
On Safari In Uganda

Travelling around Uganda you can see that many different traditions, customs, superstitions, taboos, still exist. Some are general throughout the country while others are peculiar to one tribe. Child labour is widespread in Uganda with young children performing many domestic duties. A small boy of about five years was carrying a clay pot containing water home from the well. He was seen to stop by a bush and urinate in the pot. When asked why he did this he reported that his grandmother treated him harshly, so he used to reward her by urinating in her drinking water.

A tradition which is today restricted to one tribe in Uganda is the custom of circumcision. The Bagisu people living in Mbale Region practise this ritual, which takes place every two years. Boys of suitable age are gathered together and the ceremony is carried out. One of my students invited me to witness the circumcision of his teenage son. Some young men do not wish to go through this process and escape before the appointed day. Two years later, when the time for the next circumcision ceremony approaches, those same young men again go into hiding, in fear of being caught and taken back to the home area for this traditional rite. Another of my students from the Bagisu tribe, who had so far avoided circumcision, disappeared during this traditional period until there was no longer any danger of being captured and forcibly taken home. This same man, who was over thirty years of age, had to disappear in the same way every two years. I always remember this student because after completing his training and gaining his diploma in special education, he became fully engaged in the manufacture of medicines for witch doctors.

The traditional way of carrying a baby is to have it tied on the back. This gives comfort to the child, being close to the mother, enjoying the warmth and movement of her body and it is also convenient for the mother, enabling her to continue with her household chores. Young girls playing with their dolls, made from palm or banana leaves or perhaps if living in the town, bought from a shop, will tie the doll on their backs and emulate the behaviour of the adults. I have seen toddlers of two years trying to tie a doll on their back so as to carry it around in the customary manner.

When the early explorers reached Buganda they were surprised and impressed at the level of administration found in the country. Strong religious beliefs were followed by the Baganda people, who knew that they would not have existed if there had been no god. In their understanding of god they started to praise trees, lakes, rivers and mountains. The most powerful spiritual gods were Lubale and Mayembe. They could appear in the form of snakes, lizards, as the blowing wind or in the form of human voices. These two gods had the power to kill or to prevent something bad from happening. The Baganda believed that each lake, river, hill, had some spirit responsible for its creation. The god of the sky was Kibuka Omumbale who used to shoot arrows down on to his enemies. The lake god was Mukasa Wenyanja, who required a sacrifice if you wished for a safe passage across his waters or a good catch of fish. Dungu Omuyiz was the god of hunting, who also needed a suitable offering if you wished to bring home a good supply of food. Lubale had the power to make a person ill or go mad. Each clan had to sit once or twice a year to make sacrifices to Lubale. These offerings would be in the form of goats, cows, chickens or perhaps human beings, according to the number needed to extract the amount of blood required. Lubale could speak at any time through a clan member of his choosing. Mayembe was different, being able to speak only during the hours of darkness. This spirit god could help to solve problems whenever they arose. He could help the couple who failed to get children after marriage or the man who failed to find a girl to wed. The most important act Mayembe could carry out was to heal people when they fell sick. Mayembe could arrest other spirits which did harm. After apprehending the spirit it would be tied in grass with ropes and then set ablaze, completely destroying that spirit. A sick person seeking help would be placed inside a hut in total darkness while the evil spirit was being consumed by fire outside. Family members would sit around on bark cloth, while the interpreter of Mayembe sang songs in praise of the spiritual god. Within a few minutes Mayembe would be heard raining powerful kicks at the door, bells would be ringing and speaking in tongues taking place. The way people gained help from Mayembe was to buy his favours through his clan member representative. However, before this could happen permission had to be obtained from the god Lubale, making the request and payment through his clan spokesman. Ceremonies invoking the powers of the spirit gods had to be performed in a round hut with a grass roof which was built by all clan members. In this hut you would find bark cloth, where members sat to visit their god, water, baskets of herbs and always a fire burning. When Lubale arrived the eyes of his representative would become red, he yawned frequently and might vomit. People then knew the spirit was with them and they could begin to ask their questions. The medium would begin to look at small stones, cowrie shells, old coins, to see the patterns they produced after being thrown on the ground. He would then convey the information to those seeking advice and say how to solve the problem and expel the bad spirits which were disturbing them. After receiving the information and necessary medicine people were required to pay a little money.

Different tribes have different marriage customs. In Buganda the father is responsible for seeing that his son has a hut, mats, bark cloth and pots. A dowry has to be paid which takes the form of goats, sugar, paraffin, a kanzu for the girl's father and a gomesi for the mother. Coffee beans, mushrooms, chickens, as many as ten, are given to other family members.

A sealed envelope containing money is given to the father and to aunts. After taking the bride and finding that she is a virgin, the boy's family have to provide a female goat which has never given birth. A similar thing happens if it is found that the boy has never been with a girl before. Then the bride's family have to bring a chicken to the parents of the boy. A man is never allowed to marry someone from his own clan or even marry a girl from his mother's clan.

I have travelled around in different parts of Uganda and seen a procession of cows, sheep, goats, being led along at the side of the road. Fellow passengers have told me that there is a person going to the family of his bride to hand over the bride price.

Traditionally people in Uganda protect their shadow in different ways. The shadow is looked upon as that person's spirit. The witch doctor has the power to send his spirit to take away a person's shadow. This shadow can then be interrogated by the witch doctor, who could gain any information he wished to learn about you, your family or your future plans. A way of preventing this from happening is said to be by placing a bowl of water underneath your bed or by the door so that when the witch doctor's spirit arrives to capture your shadow, it will not see the shadow because of the presence of the water. It is said that you should not abuse your shadow by trying to step on it, throw things at it or mock it in any way. I have known people to be quite happy about having their photograph taken providing you do not capture their shadow in the picture.

In the same way people are most careful what happens to the clippings from finger and toenails and hair cut from the head. Your enemy could carry these body parts to the witch doctor, who could use them to place a curse upon you. Underclothing from both men and women has to be guarded in the same way, for the same reason. Another source of trouble can be your footprint. This can be dug up, taken away and used against you to produce evil. If a person feels that someone wants to bewitch him then he is always careful not to leave any footprints when he walks along. Even the remains of an item you have eaten can be taken up and used against you. There is the documented case of an Indian man, who lived in Mbale, being told that some people wished for his death and that he must take care of his personal belongings, including his footprints, in case they were carried away. The mistake this man made was to throw down the skin of a banana he had been eating. The skin was seized and spells were made, which resulted in the man's death, so the story goes.

My only encounter with a witch doctor was when visiting a remote primary school in Mukono district. We were looking for a room to stay the night and a floor was offered in the village witch doctor's house. Through my interpreter, Charles, we spent many night hours discussing his skills and powers. He could give me a cure for my headaches. This was a leaf from one tree which was mixed and boiled with tea leaves to bring about the desired result. Yes, he could cure my sleeplessness; that was not difficult. A leaf from a different tree brushed lightly across the forehead before bed-time would do the trick. I asked if a person came to him wishing to kill an enemy, would he perform the task? A simple task to fulfil, was his answer, providing the necessary money was paid. This discussion I took a little further and asked if I was a local teacher and had a problem with my

164

headmaster and wanted him dead, could he carry out this act for me? Again he confirmed that this was an easy piece of work for a man of his skills. Would he like to tell my fortune? I asked. He agreed but not until the following morning because he would have to escort us to his round hut or spirit house for an accurate reading.

At the appointed time Charles and I followed our witch doctor to his special consulting room, which must be round and have a thatched roof. Apparently spirits will not enter a hut through a modern roof of tin or tiles. Bark cloth draped the interior walls and a number of spears and animal skins were scattered about. The three of us sat cross-legged on the floor. From a small bark cloth bag he threw a mixture of shells, bones, coloured stones and pieces of metal on to the floor. These items he gathered in his hand, only to throw them down again, each time noting the patterns they formed. First my fortune was examined. Our friend told me certain things which would happen to me, my mother and to one of my college students. All he said came true. Mention was made of a friend and particularly her eating habits. This knowledge he could not possibly have known in the normal way but somehow he had this information. Charles was next to have his future life examined and he also found most of his information to be correct. We later heard that this witch doctor had inherited these special powers from his mother. From a later meeting with his brother I discovered that our friend had a disabled son, something which his greatest powers could not prevent or heal.

To understand more about life in a rural community I recommend a visit to one of the village halls when a play is being performed or a programme of song and dance is presented. Last night we went to our local community centre in the village of Kikubampanga. The size of the building was similar to that of the average village hall in England, but there the similarity ended. No seats were provided inside the room, which had a mud floor, window frames covered by sacks and all illuminated by a single eighty-watt bulb. You take your own chairs and on paying for entry a lady with a rubber stamp and ink-pad stamps your palm. Starting time for the Gólden Star Singers was 7.30 p.m., the time we arrived. Better not go too early warned Charles, usually these shows start late. The time approached 8.30 p.m. and just the two of us sat on our own bench, while a solitary member of the company banged out a few tunes on two home-made drums, to let us know that something was about to happen and not to give up and demand the return of our money. By 9.30 p.m. the audience had doubled to four, so now the situation looked slightly more promising. The following fifteen minutes showed a dramatic increase in numbers, there were seven of us, all voicing our impatience and holding up our palms to show that we had paid for an evening's entertainment. The entrance price was the equivalent of two days' wages for the average working person in that area. Just before 10 p.m. the same audience of seven stood for the national anthem. The head count at 10.30 p.m. numbered eighteen, which included seven children, who did not pay to enter, and a drunk. This man might not have paid but perhaps his contribution was the dance which he performed around us, which occupied some of my attention when the signing stopped and dialogue followed in Luganda, which I could not follow. At 11.30 p.m. the number had increased to twenty-three, which now included eight children and two drunks, who danced together. Midnight came and the Golden Stars were still full of song. The themes followed topical events, singing about poverty, prostitution, AIDS, unfaithful husbands, things which a girl should know before marriage. I noticed how quietly the children sat throughout the long night, attentive to all songs, music and short sketches. Even the two babies did not let out a single cry.

The final item on the programme was a musical play, which included night-dancers. These are the spirits which roam around during the hours of darkness, usually naked, and perform evil acts, such as stealing and eating dead bodies. For this performance the single light bulb was removed. Half a dozen semi-naked players pranced around the audience, pushing into our faces what were supposed to be dead bodies, while torch lights flashed on and off and the drummer continued to bang violently away on his drum. Excited, amused or frightened, depending on the age-group, the audience stood once again for the national anthem as the show came to an end at 1 a.m. We stiffly marched out into the cold, misty night, with aching backs and bottoms, to begin our walk home, wondering if we would see any more naked night-dancers appearing out of the mist before we reached our cold, unlit house and disappeared under the mosquito nets to sleep.

When I was a student attending primary school in Queensland, in the 1950s, I was one of a class of seventy-two children, sitting seven to a bench and writing on slates. My parents thought those conditions were primitive compared with the school I had left in England. That

Australian experience was sheer luxury when I see schools here in Uganda.

In Tororo Region I went into a classroom where the teacher had ingeniously formed mounds of mud to produce working surfaces, where children could kneel throughout a lesson and have a ledge on which to place their books. A school in Mukono district had half a roof for each classroom which meant that at least half the school day children could sit in the shade and all take shelter from the rain. I did read of two disabled children in another country dying from sun stroke because all lessons took place outside without even a tree for shelter. A school I looked at in Mipigi Region had stones and branches as the only seating the school provided. Parents sometimes punish their children for arriving home with a dirty school uniform but this is usually after a child has sat on a floor of mud throughout the long school day. The top school in Busia district, charging the highest school fees in that area, has an average of one hundred and fourteen children in each primary class. The Ministry of Education recommends a class size of forty pupils. I saw one class at a school in Iganga district which had one hundred and twenty-three children in one room and this number included eleven physically disabled pupils who sat on the floor at the front. Some children run to school early each day to claim a seat on one of two benches provided in the classroom. Many classes are held under trees with children sitting on the grass. How romantic, one American woman said when she saw this, but perhaps she did not think of the ants, the sun and rain and the terrible effect this has on the development of a child's handwriting. One headmaster boasted that before he joined the school three years before the children all sat on the mud floor. His contribution to the school had been to provide pieces of rock for each child to sit on in class. Nearly fifty per cent of children drop out of school due to parents being unable to pay the average £6 per pupil per term. To add to this pitiful state of affairs there is also a great lack of scholastic materials in schools and a large number of unqualified teachers.

A report from a mission school in Buganda written in 1881 stated: "The Baganda are very eager pupils and are besides very clever at learning to read and write. As a rule it only took the teacher a couple of months to teach the younger lads to read fluently, although they did not even know the alphabet at the beginning of that time." Today with a primary school enrolment of thirty-eight per cent for girls and sixty-two per cent for boys and with adult literacy rate of forty-four per cent for women and sixty-two per cent for men, the early potential shown in 1881 has not been allowed to flourish.

When travelling the roads of Uganda, driving or on foot, great care must be taken to look out for cyclists and the loads they carry. This is even more necessary at night, because less than one per cent of bicycles carry front or rear lights. Many an evening I have been walking at the side of a road or track and have almost been tangled up with a bicycle and its rider. I have seen myself or bicycle more than once go off the road into a ditch. African nights appear far darker than in Europe, due to country roads being without streetlights and houses not having the electricity which brightens most country areas in Europe.

It is fascinating to see the size, amount and variety of goods transported by the common bicycle. Recently I spotted a settee plus two matching armchairs with ten cushions all being carried on one bicycle. It is not unusual to see a double bed travelling along complete with mattress. These machines must be strong, because they carry as many as four twenty-litre jerrycans of water plus the driver. I can just about lift a full hank containing around eighty bananas. The cyclist does not appear to have too much difficulty in transporting five hanks, twenty or thirty miles to the markets of Kampala. When driving I am not too happy coming across a cyclist carrying sugar cane. The sticks stretch out almost to the centre of the road. Great care has to be taken to slow down, while watching other vehicles approaching in both directions; also, to look for the next pothole and hope that the cyclist carrying the sugar cane will heed your warning horn and move slightly to the left to allow you a safe passage. I do not know how more sugar cane haulers are not seriously injured and their machines destroyed when you see how a taxi, truck or bus speeds past, with horn blaring but making no effort to reduce speed. In the town of Mbale I once saw a cyclist riding along carrying a plank of wood so wide on the back of his bicycle that it took up the whole width of the road. We crawled along slowly behind until we could drive off on a different road.

Our neighbours in Kakiri were recently extending their house. One morning I was sitting outside reading and also watching the twenty-five house bricks, which would keep arriving, all strapped on to the back of a bicycle, stacked in neat piles of five. When people are transporting grass their machine takes on the appearance of a huge hay stack majestically gliding along. In southern Uganda ladies do not ride bicycles; this form of transport is reserved for men. If a woman does wish to use a bicycle, then she is always sitting side-saddle behind the man. In some towns you can hire a bicycle taxi. These bikes have a padded passenger seat and you will be driven some miles for a few hundred shillings. I used to take this means of travel when visiting schools in Iganga district. Perhaps one of the strangest sights to western eyes is to see the cyclist or passenger going along holding an umbrella, but these umbrellas are the large leaves of the banana plant, which do give reasonable shelter from light showers.

When attending orientation courses in developing countries I have always been warned about risks associated with any motoring accident in which we might become involved. We are told that if we drive and hit a pedestrian, never stop, whatever the condition of the victim, but to drive to the nearest police station and report the accident. The reason for this is that as soon as a road accident occurs, people will leave their work, houses, market stalls or their own vehicles and rush excitedly to the scene. Friends and relations of the injured person might arrive in a shocked condition and quickly begin to attack the driver and passengers.

Fortunately this situation has not happened to me in Africa; but when travelling in Bangladesh, in a Land-Rover driven by the English wife of the manager of a factory producing fertiliser, an ugly event took place. Returning from a tour of the district my friend drove into a home-made bicycle rickshaw, turning over the contraption and slightly injuring the cyclist. A crowd ran shouting to the scene. We drove off but were chased by a large group seeking revenge. We slowed down as we approached a congested area, which allowed time for the growing crowd to reach us. Stones broke the lights and some windows while other members of the mob tried to turn the vehicle over by rocking it from side to side. Luckily for us the traffic ahead cleared just in time, allowing us to hurry back to the security of the compound, where my friend telephoned to report the matter to the police.

Last year, when returning to Kampala along the Bomba Road, we came across an accident where an elderly lady was stretched out in the road. People had gathered at the scene and two Europeans waved for us to stop. They explained that the lady had run in front of their car and she might be dead. Fortunately traffic police happened to arrive at the scene and the lady seemed to make a quick recovery. We left the driver to solve his problem with the police but took his companion and the old lady to the hospital.

Late one night we were driving between Mbarara and Kabale, when we came across a bicycle and rider lying in the centre of the road. I advised Charles not to stop because this might have been a trap. Friends of the cyclist could have been hiding in the bushes to attack some helpful motorist. We drove around the obstruction and went on our way. This might have been a genuine case of someone really needing our assistance but you can never take the risk.

We came across one man who had been hit by a car. He was lying at the side of the road with friends around trying to give help. Although he had not really been injured, he believed he was dying because of his psychological state. From his previous experience he knew that when a person was hit by a vehicle he died, therefore because of his minor bump, he had to die. It took a hospital doctor a long time to convince this man that hospital medicine would cure his injury and the man survived. In similar cases people have died.

I read recently in one of our newspapers about corruption taking place in the police force. The president had received numerous complaints from the business community saying that the traffic police were corrupt. The president had the police removed from the national roads and city streets and restricted them to police stations for a short period while internal investigations took place. We have faced this same problem when travelling around Uganda. Driving home at night from Hoima we turned a bend in the road to find we were in the middle of a police road block. Because we had gone over their mark in the road we had to pay a large fine or lose the car. Due to the dark and the bend of the road it would have been difficult for us to have pulled up any sooner. We have been stopped a number of times by traffic police wanting money to buy a meal. They tell you that your tyres are worn or some other part of the vehicle requires attention. You know this is not true but hand over the money or your car would be confiscated and you left stranded at the side of the road. This situation is worse in Kenya, where we found traffic police would point their gun at you through the car window as well as demand money for contravening some imaginary traffic rule. Their answer to this is that they have to eat, you have money so why should they not have a share of it?

In 1995 we drove along the road from Fort Portal to Bundibugyo, making for the crossing with Zaire, when we reached Sempaya hot springs. At the road junction for the springs we saw another sign which directed us to Burondo village camp, the home of a group of pygmies. These families had been removed from Mpulya forest, which was their natural habitat and resettled at Buronda. Their old home, and the reason for their removal, is now Semuliki National Park. Standing by the sign pointing to the settlement, were a few pygmy men and children. They eagerly invited us to visit their new village and when we showed interest, climbed into the back of our pick-up and gave directions. Once we were in their camp we were trapped. They demanded a large sum of money for entering their village. If we wanted to take photographs, see any dancing, hear traditional songs, look at artefacts or enter their huts, again a high price was required. When I saw their behaviour I wanted no further dealings with them and wished for a hasty retreat. Charles was more cautious and said we were in a difficult situation with the pygmies having us at their mercy and we would not be allowed to leave with the vehicle unless we handed over some money. I became more aware of the spears and bows and arrows being carried and that many pygmies had clambered into our truck with others crowding around us. I had to admit that Charles was right. We eventually escaped by paying an entrance fee plus buying some of their handicraft. I did notice that they were living in squalid conditions and thought that their huts, made entirely of tin, were unsuitable for the hot climate; we were not many miles from the equator.

Perhaps a reason for their hostility is the way they have been treated by the authorities in recent years. This year (1996) I have been reading press reports saying that the pygmies in the same Burondo resettlement camp have been dying. A member of parliament said when the pygmies were persuaded by the Adventist Development and Relief Agency to come out of the forest, their natural habitat, to the resettlement camp, they started dying and eventually started destroying the houses they were put in and sold items they were given, such as hoes and blankets and then went back into the forest The director of the Uganda Wildlife Authority said that what ADRA was doing to re-settle the pygmies was pathetic. He said the so-called houses, which were tents made from iron sheets, were too small, lacking windows and ventilation. He accused the agency of removing the pygmies from the forest and pushing them into an environment which was alien to them. Another official stated that creating national parks was displacing and endangering lives of forest based communities, such as the pygmies. He continued by saying when pygmies were forced out of the forest they had found themselves in a situation of hopelessness and had resorted to over-drinking, selling sex and to smoking drugs.

Fort Portal was recently in the news, being the place where the coronation was held for the new omukama of Toro, King Oyo. Toro is one of the four kingdoms which form part of present-day Uganda. The new king inherited the title when he was just three years of age. In 1996 he performed the last ritual to become the traditional head of the kingdom, when he formally closed his late father's tomb. This ceremony had to be performed by the child-king before celebrating his first coronation anniversary. As part of this ceremony he gave orders for his late father's servants to surrender all instruments of power. Young King Oyo later returned to England, where he attends a nursery school in London.

If you walk around any of the larger Ugandan towns, Masaka, Mbarara, Kabale, Kampala, Jinja, Mabale, early in the morning you will see the street children of this country. They will be emerging from their overnight sleeping places, which might be the inside of large water or drainage pipes, an abandoned vehicle, the side of a rubbish skip, under a plastic or cardboard covering or beneath a bush. Shop doorways and inside empty or bombed buildings is another favourite place of refuge. The urchins, boys and girls aged from about five to early teens will start to gather food for their morning snack, as soon as the sun begins to rise. This breakfast might be gleaned from leftovers found around the market, scraps put out by local restaurants or items discovered on rubbish dumps, where youngsters scavenge for food along with stray dogs, scratching chickens, ever-hungry pigs, diseased rats, squabbling crows and the ungainly marabou storks. I have seen street children collect dry material, palm leaves, paper, grass, to build a fire on which they cook their gathered scraps in a rusty tin which might have once contained the luxury of baked beans, tinned fruit or jam. When their meagre meal is eaten they will set out to see what can be begged, borrowed, collected or stolen. Some children will be caught and ill used by the police. Others might be beaten, even killed by an angry mob after being caught stealing, or end up in a fight with one of their fellow conspirators. Some will even earn money through prostitution or by selling illicit home brewed alcohol or drugs.

Where do these street children come from and what makes them have to suffer this existence of having a daily struggle to survive? At one time they would mainly consist of orphans, whose parents had died in one of the many civil wars which have taken place in Uganda, since the country gained its independence in 1962. Today the main cause is the parents' having died of AIDS. In one area, close to the border with Tanzania, the number of adults who have died from AIDS has reached around fifty per cent. Some of these destitute children will be refugees coming from civil wars in neighbouring Rwanda and the Sudan or from fighting which is taking place across the border in Zaire. Another cause of children having to exist on the streets is due to the family having driven the child away from the home. This happens when a child is born to the second, third or fourth wife of a marriage and then the father dies. The first or senior wife might not want the children of other wives living in the same house, so out they must go to fend for themselves. This also happens when a man loses or leaves his wife and takes a new woman to his home. This new companion sometimes does not want the children of a previous marriage staying in the same house so she forces the father to drive his own children from the family home, making them depart for a life on the streets.

These unfortunate street children have been receiving some practical help and hope for the future from a number of overseas, non-governmental organisations. The African Development Society, with its head office in Germany, has been assisting an orphanage located just outside Kampala's city limits. This centre is presently taking care of more than eighty children, some of whom are from Rwanda. Child Restoration Outreach, started by a Dutch lady, is helping street children in Mbale. Children can enter their building on a daily basis to receive a meal, a bath, clothing and counselling. Last year CRO had one hundred and twenty-six children belonging to the project. The same organisation has a rehabilitation school with thirty-five boys and twenty girls. International Care and Relief, a British based charity, is helping children in Rakai district. Aid workers think that as many as one hundred thousand children have been orphaned in that area alone by both parents dying from AIDS. An encouraging story was recently reported in the sports press about a football team made up of Kampala street children. Team members received a complete set of football kit from a Leicestershire-based youth project, Response Ability and Environmental Leadership Alliance, which tries to promote community awareness among young people. The children earned their kit by participating in an environmental cleaning exercise in some of the main public areas of Kampala.

Elderly people in Africa have traditionally been given great prestige by the younger generations of children and grandchildren. Their wisdom, experience, curses, were respected or feared. Today, since the spread of AIDS throughout Uganda and the neighbouring countries, this prestigious position which the elderly once enjoyed has now gone due to a missing generation. Whereas before the old were both revered and cared for, today they have lost all or many of their sons and daughters. If the wife of a son is still alive she is probably also battling with AIDS. This leaves the grandmother as perhaps the only adult in the immediate family who is available to care for the grandchildren. Instead of cherishing her peaceful years of retirement, she finds that she has to work even harder to keep both herself and her grandchildren from starving.

A custom which is still followed in Uganda is when a man dies his wife will go to live with her husband's next youngest brother to be one of his wives. Her children will also join this new larger family. If a man loses his wife he will often take home with him, after the funeral, a younger sister of his wife to give him company during what would be his lonely nights. This is until the man finds a new wife for himself, which does not seem to take very long. I am not sure what the sister-in-law's husband thinks about this situation, but it is the custom.

Coffee was introduced into Uganda at the beginning of this century and quickly became the country's main export crop. Uganda had been the largest producer of coffee in the Commonwealth. Many small farmers base their income on the coffee bean. Today coffee brings in about eighty per cent of Uganda's export earnings. Due to constant fluctuations in prices on the world coffee market some farmers have lost money and decided to uproot their plants and try other crops. Two newly-introduced crops are strawberries and roses. Planting the local variety of coffee means a long wait of six years before the tree matures and produces its first crop of beans. This is an experience which Karen Blixen shared with us in her book, *Out of Africa*. Today there is a newly-introduced variety of coffee which will mature within two years of planting. Many country people with a small plot of land will grow a few coffee plants for their own consumption. Making visits to a friend working in a coffee factory in the town of Bomba, I have often found the works closed, with the manager waiting for the seasonal crop to be ready for harvesting again before he can recruit new workers. When the sacks of beans arrive at the factory, from neighbouring farms, then plenty of hands are required, with unloading, roasting, sorting, which is carried out by hand, one bean at a time, and the final re-sacking until the consignment is ready to continue its journey around the world. The husks from the beans, which used to be thrown away as waste, are now used as a valuable fertiliser, especially for the banana plantation.

A new discovery in Uganda is something which is being called 'The Wonder Plant'. This is the African soap berry. In Ethiopia it is grown for commercial purposes and even exported as a detergent. This soap berry could become a successful cash crop as a raw material for detergents and pharmaceutical products. The plant has been used by local people over many years but now scientists are studying its potential for making a detergent, for controlling bilharzia and as a cure for liver flukes in cattle. Early results show that Uganda could follow the success which Ethiopia has achieved with the soap berry, producing an alternative to the conventionally produced detergents. We are told that the product in Uganda, so far produced, still needs certain additives to improve the quality and quantity of its foam, which will satisfy the housewife. The African soap berry could become an important cash crop for the small farmer which would give him an additional income to the present traditionally grown crops.

The cotton industry has been in decline since it reached its peak twenty-five years ago. At that time Uganda was producing around half a million bales of cotton per year. There are still more than forty ginneries to be found scattered all over the country but most farmers have turned to more profitable sources of income.

When passing a neighbour's house I could always smell fermenting fruit, which reminded me of a corner of my old back garden in England, where I used to throw the windfalls from our cooking apple trees. There they would remain to be pecked at by birds, eaten by worms or rot into the ground over the winter months. Knowing that apples did not grow in this part of the world, I started to peer through the neighbour's banana plantation to try to trace the cause of the smell but the only unusual items I could spot were wooden canoes scattered around the house. We are far from the nearest stretch of open water, so this added to the puzzle. I also noticed, just as it was getting dark, men walking into the compound, only to stagger out late at night. Charles explained the mystery. This banana plantation grew a special type of banana, locally called kayinja or plantain. These are for making home-brewed banana beer, often produced by the women but enjoyed in its final form by men. Beer-making plantains are picked and placed in a pit, covered with leaves from the same plant, plus soil, and left for three days to begin the fermenting process. The earth is then removed and after a further three days the fruit is taken out, peeled and placed with grass in a beer canoe. Now the men play their part and trample on the fruit to extract the juice. Sorghum flour is added and the mixture left in a second beer canoe for another day to ferment again before it is strained into gourds for drinking. The old men say that their elders always poured a little beer on the ground before they themselves drank, because they always remembered the spirits of those ancestors down below. Personally I prefer to use our extra bananas, with a little lime-juice and sugar, to make banana jam. Each week I would use six bananas, with the other ingredients, to produce two full jars.

I have seen a different way of drinking home-produced brew in the regions of Pallisa and Mbale. Adults gather around a large clay pot and suck out the contents through a long tube which has a mouth piece at the end, rather like men in the Middle East who sit around and smoke from a hookah. In the same way the tube is passed from mouth to mouth around the group, each taking a series of gulps lasting about fifteen seconds. This practice continues until the pot is empty or until members fall out of the circle. When staying with a family in Mbale, who knew my drinking habits, they enjoyed their customary evening drink while I sat in an armchair nearby enjoying my own pot of tea.

Some people, when travelling abroad, fear to say no to food or drink when offered, anxious not to offend their hosts. Not taking alcohol myself, I always refuse and have never met any hostility at my decision; my choice has always been accepted.

Driving along the main road between the town of Masaka and the capital Kampala, we always see men holding up large fish for sale to passing motorists. This road runs close to Lake Victoria and the fish being sold are either tilapia of Nile perch. My favourite meal is steamed tilapia served with matoke, the staple diet for people in southern Uganda. Matoke is another type of banana which is boiled and mashed before eaten, the modern way of cooking the dish. The traditional way is to slowly steam the fruit, which is wrapped and tied up in banana leaves, placed in a suferia, (a large saucepan without handles) and left for about three hours until soft. Nile perch is a rather fatty fish and does not agree with my digestion. Unfortunately some clever people thought they would add Nile perch to the waters of Lake Victoria to supplement the indigenous tilapia. One fact about these perch, which was not understood, is that they eat other fish and when that supply runs out they happily eat each other. The result of this of course is that tilapia are becoming more difficult to find and more expensive to buy.

Along the roads further away from the lake, small pick-up trucks are seen at around ten o'clock each morning, moving from village to village selling fish. The unusual thing about this is that although the fish is of a good size, there is nothing to eat between head and tail; the two are joined by one fleshless backbone. It looks as though these fish have been attacked by shoal of hungry piranhas. However, the real reason is that all flesh is removed from the fish which is then taken for export and the poor village people in this area have just the head, tail and backbone to buy, the parts which are not wanted by customers overseas.

When eating out I rarely order meat. So often in the past I have been caught with this uneatable meal. The problem is that tough meat or old cow in Uganda requires plenty of cooking. Three hours is the minimum boiling time before my teeth can manage to break the meat into pieces small enough to swallow. I find it impossible to consume the large chunks of partly-cooked beef the way Ugandan men seem to manage. This situation is not quite so bad when eating in a restaurant and you are the customer paying for the food and can, as I often do, take the leather-like substance away in a bag to give to my dog, Cobra. But the situation becomes embarrassing when being entertained by a friend. If you left their meat on your plate and said you were going to take it home for your dog, it would be looked upon as a great insult and you would never be invited back for another meal. If the meat is no longer fresh and its smell signals to you its deteriorating condition then it can be boiled for nine hours, so I am told, and will be safe to eat. At least in this well-cooked state it should be tender enough even for my old teeth to chew.

One evening I was walking with a friend to Kakiri when we came across four small children sitting around a termite's nest waiting for these insects to show themselves above ground and begin their flying courtship. When the swarming began eager hands moved, alternately placing a termite in their collecting jar and one into their mouths, including the fluttering wings, to suck and crunch, enjoying the sweet taste which oozes from the body of this type of termite. I suppose these titbits might be looked upon as a free substitute for sweets, which are not readily available in the small towns. Also the termite is more nutritious if we think of its food value. I rejected these wriggling creatures, which the youngsters offered to me to eat, but my companion did enjoy eating a handful. When swarming time approaches people build a rough shelter of sticks over the smaller nests and keep watch until the insects emerge. A cloth is then placed over the sticks so as to prevent any escaping. In this way all will be captured to provide a tasty bed-time snack. That same evening the fireflies were active, making some trees sparkle like illuminated Christmas trees.

When living abroad a constant source of stomach upsets is unclean drinking water. When buying soft drinks I always order one without ice. Sometimes the drink will arrive with ice but this I refuse to accept. I remember a barman in the departure lounge at Antigua Airport was so busy playing with his computer game that he did not listen to my request and presented me with a drink plus ice. Realising his mistake he dipped his fingers into my lemonade and removed one piece of ice at a time. Another drink I avoid is one which has to be diluted with water. The water will often come straight from a tap or bucket without first being boiled and filtered. In different parts of Uganda our drinking water has come from wells, lakes, rivers, natural springs and swamps. All this water has to be boiled for at least five minutes, poured into a commercially manufactured water filter, before we can use the filtered water for drinking and cooking. Twice each week the filters have to be removed and the film of mud scrubbed off. Some people filter their water first then boil but I do not like the idea of a collection of parasites living inside my water filter. Other people try to solve this daily water problem by purchasing bottled mineral water. Recently in Uganda newspapers have warned against buying the main locally-produced brand because it failed to meet required health and safety standards. Undergoing laboratory tests a consignment was found to contain solid particles, which prevented the complete killing of bacteria and instead acted as a home for bacteria to multiply. I will keep to my five minutes of boiling and filtering.

Tourism, which used to be Uganda's fourth largest source of foreign exchange until the civil wars which followed independence, is now being revived, with emphasis being placed on ecotourism. It is estimated that eighty per cent of tourists arriving in Uganda today come with the aim of visiting the mountain gorilla. Uganda is the home of about two thirds of these rare mountain primates. With Zaire and Rwanda now being more difficult to visit, Uganda is the place people travel to for a glimpse of these noble creatures. Kabale, which is reached via Masaka and Mbarara, is the nearest town to Bwindi Impenetrable Forest, the starting point for the gorilla trek. Two families have now become accustomed to being approached by humans and having their photographs taken. Bwindi Forest Reserve was given National Park status in 1992, when the government realised how the area could become an earner of foreign currency. To enter the park there is a charge of one hundred and twenty-five US dollars per person, the latest figure I was quoted. Creating a national park does impinge on the rights of local people who use the forest but efforts are being made by some park authorities to see that people do receive tangible benefits from tourism.

There is not the wildlife to see in Uganda that there was during the 1960s. Idi Amin used to enjoy taking his friends to visit Queen Elizabeth Game Park to hunt animals. Most of the wildlife of this park was hunted to near extinction. During the civil wars local people used to kill animals to eat because of the food shortage. The elephant population of the Queen Elizabeth Park, which used to number four thousand animals, declined to around four hundred. This park is an excellent place to see the hippopotamus, especially when you take a boat trip across the lake to see these massively built, semi-aquatic mammals rising from the water all around you, close enough to touch. Being gregarious by nature it is fairly easy to film a collection of large heads, with wide-open mouths, showing a fierce display of incisors and canines which we are told grow continuously. Travelling through other areas of the park you can drive mile upon mile and see little apart from different species of antelope.

Jijja is the second largest town in Uganda built around the place John Speke identified as the source of the River Nile, flowing out from the inland sea of Lake Victoria. Herodotus (c.485–425 BC), the Greek historian, traced the source of the Nile to three great lakes in the interior of Africa. From his time until the middle of the seventeenth century, these three lakes have regularly appeared on maps of the Dark Continent, as it was then called. The word Jinja means stone. Jinja was the place where many stones could be found. The town became a growing industrial centre with the inauguration of the Owen Falls Dam in 1954. The power generated at Owen Falls, one of the keys to Uganda's industrial development, supplies much of urban Uganda with electricity and surplus power is exported to Kenya and Tanzania. Jinja is typical of many towns which have developed around the world where Indian communities have settled. We see many attractive, single storey buildings, fairly wide tree-lined avenues, parks and open spaces. Since the ousting of the Asians by Idi Amin, the town has taken on a dejected appearance. At the turn of this century it was seen how communications would be made easier by the construction of a railway. This rail network was largely built by workers brought from India. After its completion many stayed and other Indians emigrated to live and establish businesses in East Africa. Jinja was largely developed by its Indian community. Close to the source of the Nile stands a Hindu temple with a statue of Mahatma Gandhi in the grounds. The statue is in memory of Gandhi's wish to have his ashes scattered in the River Nile. All that can be seen of the source of the Nile today is water flowing over a line of concrete blocks, behind a chain link wire fence. On the opposite bank stands an obelisk marking the spot where Speke was supposed to have stood when he realised his discovery.

When the River Nile leaves Lake Victoria it flows through the Bujagali Falls, a favourite picnic site, and continues through Lake Kyoga to Lake Albert. This part of the river is called the Victoria Nile. From Lake Albert the river drops one hundred and thirty feet through the impressive gorge at Kabalega, or Murchinson Falls, which is a national park. Kabalega was the leader of Bunyoro one hundred years ago and fought against Buganda and the British administration over a period of years. He was defeated in 1893 by a force of Bagandan fighters, led by Major Owens, and fled into exile.

Driving time from Kampala to Jinja does not take much more than one hour, travelling along a good road and passing patches of dense forest, with picnic areas at the side of the road. This can be a pleasant day's outing from the capital with visits to Jinja Town, the dam, source of the Nile and the Bujagali Falls. A few years ago we took our lunch to Bujagali and sat watching boys ride the falls on jerrycans, women busy with their weekly wash of clothes and young people swimming. Care needs to be taken where you sit because dangers can be close at hand. We took the precaution of sitting on a sheet but at some stage of the meal I must have placed my hand on the grass. The following week we flew to Tanzania to begin a five country African safari. While staying with Assay in Dar es Salaam I felt an itch at the end of my right index finger with a small white patch at the tip. This irritation started to swell and continued with a slowly moving red line extending along the finger and across the hand. When we reached Egha's house in Mbeya, his wife, who is a nurse, said I had a jigger which needed cutting out. She carried out this operation fairly quickly, removing pieces of worm. The dressing was changed three days running. A week later staying at the Victoria Falls Hotel in Zimbabwe, I still felt the sensation of something crawling up the inside of my arm but the hotel nurse said there was nothing to worry about. Today I am left with a tiny scar to remember this creeping eruption as it is sometimes called. The trouble probably came from a hookworm larvae dropped from a cat or dog. *Larvae migrans* are contracted by walking with bare feet on ground which has been contaminated by animal faeces. In my case it was the hand which came into contact with this parasite. This incident reminds me of a precaution I have always taken when travelling abroad, in Europe as well as tropical countries. I never go barefoot in any wet area, bathroom, showers, or around the house, both inside or out. My feet are covered in the shower by flip flops and by leather sandals in other places.

Another trip we enjoyed was a weekend in Tororo, where we climbed to the top of the hill which dominates the town. Permission should be gained from the town police station before the climb can begin. Three of us set off to reach the top but one of the group gave up half way, a man half my age. Kisoro town, close to the border with Rwanda is very different from the landscape and people met in eastern Uganda. Visits were made to markets, two hospitals and a training school for nurses, where I gave some lectures. All men and boys over the age of about five years walk in this area carrying a stick. Tea plantations and factories in the Mityana district were the source of a number of memorable photographs. One area I have been wanting to visit is the vast Karamoja Region in northern Uganda, bordering on to Sudan. So far I have been prevented from making this journey due to security problems. People in Karamoja live in semi-desert surroundings, keeping cattle and dressing in a different way from all other people in Uganda. The traditional tribal dress of the Karamojong, which is widely worn today, is their birthday suit. Here we find it the same as with all other clothing, it wears, creases and wrinkles with age.

Conclusion

I have now retired from many years of teaching and teacher training in different parts of the world.

It gives me great pleasure when I receive correspondence from my ex-students, detailing their progress in the field of special education. Letters continue to arrive from class teachers, school principals, college lecturers, a deputy director, school inspectors and an educational adviser, working in a number of developing countries. Some seek advice, others ask for help or give me welcome news of their school, life and family. I never cease to be amazed when I hear of the number of children, particularly in Africa, who have been given my name. It brings much satisfaction when I remember the role I played in their education and training.

Two student friends who feature in this book are Assay in Tanzania and Charles in Uganda. They are both married with their own family. Assay is now working as an audiologist in Dar es Salaam, after completing a course of further training in England. Charles is currently director of Kojcha School for the Deaf in Uganda.

My wish is that I will be able to continue the support and encouragement which I have previously given for many more years. The difference now is this help will have to come mainly from my home base in England, with perhaps an occasional overseas educational visit. During my years of retirement I hope to maintain a programme of travel around the world, noting the odd, the unusual and the interesting, with the idea of recalling some of these tales in future books.

Kojcha School for the Deaf

The main school I have referred to in this book is Kojcha School for the Deaf in Uganda.

This is a private residential school for children who are profoundly deaf. A few pupils have an additional disability and some are orphans. Kojcha School opened in May 1995 with one deaf, physically disabled boy. The number of pupils has increased to twenty-five at the end of 1996. We have a waiting list of deaf children wishing to join our school but at present the residential and day accommodation will not cater for a larger number. At the time of writing we are trying to complete our first permanent building. Although three classes are being taught in this new block, we are waiting to fit doors and windows, ceilings and floors and to plaster and paint the walls.

Kojcha School for the Deaf is registered at the Ministry of Education in Kampala and we have received a licence to operate but no financial help is given by the government or from any local or overseas organisation. Few parents are able to pay the school fees. Last year we established a small group of 'Friends of Kojcha School for the Deaf'. Some friends have made donations to the school which helps us with the school feeding programme. More friends are needed so that we can extend our accommodation and reach our target of providing residential accommodation for two hundred profoundly deaf children from nursery through to secondary education.

Further information and a school newsletter can be obtained from:

The Director, Charles H. Sseggendo
Kojcha School for the Deaf
PO Box ███ 22737
Kampala
Uganda.

Index

A